Albert Frederick Calvert

Western Australia and Its Welfare

A reproduction of articles which have appeared in the West Australian review,

1893-1894

Albert Frederick Calvert

Western Australia and Its Welfare
A reproduction of articles which have appeared in the West Australian review, 1893-1894

ISBN/EAN: 9783337312213

Printed in Europe, USA, Canada, Australia, Japan

Cover: Foto ©ninafisch / pixelio.de

More available books at **www.hansebooks.com**

WESTERN AUSTRALIA AND ITS WELFARE.

A REPRODUCTION OF ARTICLES WHICH HAVE APPEARED IN

THE WEST AUSTRALIAN REVIEW,
1893—1894.

BY

ALBERT F. CALVERT.

LONDON:
SIMPKIN, MARSHALL, HAMILTON, KENT & CO., LIMITED.
1895.

PRINTED BY WALTERS & CO.,
WESTON-SUPER-MARE.

PREFACE.

MANY of the readers of the *West Australian Review* may not be aware that it started its career under the title of *Calvert's West Australian Mining Register* in September, 1893. For some years I had taken a very deep interest in the mineral resources of the colony, and had written a few books upon this and kindred subjects. Encouraged by the favourable notices which my efforts called forth, and foreseeing that the gold fields were destined at a very early date to proclaim their great importance to the investing public, I resolved to depart from the ordinary traditions of journalism and issue a weekly paper devoted exclusively to the discussion of Western Australian topics. The colony being so distant, so obscure, and so utterly unfamiliar to the large majority of English readers, it was pointed out to me that such a paper, published in London, could not hope to succeed. Even the larger and more important Australian colonies were content with one journal, which represented their interests collectively; it was not therefore to be supposed that a West Australian organ, pure and simple, would meet with adequate acceptance or encouragement.

Nevertheless I launched the *Review* in unpretentious form—not without misgivings it is true—but firmly evinced that before many months had passed, the name of Western Australia would be as well known in the metropolis of the world as even South Africa, in spite of the unexampled advantages of free advertisement, possessed by the latter colony. Within six months' time £35,000 worth of quartz and gold from Bayley's Reward Claim was exhibited in the City and West End of London. Then came news of other great discoveries, followed by what has been called the "West Australian Boom." This has all occurred *since* I started the humble *Register*, whether, or how far, it contributed to this result it is not for me to say.

After running for six months under the above title, for reasons which are immaterial, the paper became the *West Australian Review*, having by this time a largely increased circle of readers, both in the United Kingdom and the Colonies. It was recently suggested to me that many of the earlier articles which appeared in the *Register* and the *Review* before Westralia's notoriety was established would be worthy of reproduction in a concise form. The following pages have therefore been compiled from the issues of 1893-94; and will be found to contain both prophecies and commentaries on the passing ev of the most important epoch of Western Australia's history.

ALBERT F. CALVERT.

Authors' Club, S.W.,
       January, 1895.

CONTENTS.

I.—Concerning our Objects . . . 1
II.—Concerning Difficulties and Dangers . . 3
III.—Westralia's Minerals: A Retrospect . . 7
IV.—Early Gold Discovery 12
IV.—Concerning other Mineral Resources . . 24
V.—Relics of a Sunken Wreck 28
VI.—A Plea for Specimens at the Imperial Institute 34
VII.—Concerning the Homesteads Act . . 38
VIII.—Albert F. Calvert at the Royal Colonial Institute 42
IX.—A Momentous Question: Water . . . 46
X.—Concerning our Change of Name . . . 53
XI.—A Noble Specimen of Westralia's Wealth . 56
XII.—Bars and Quartz for the Imperial Institute 62
XIII.—Gold to the Rescue: A Comparison . 64
XIV.—Shall Westralia Federate? . . . 68
XV.—United we Stand 72
XVI.—The Institute of Mining Engineers Seek Information 76
XVII.—A United Australia 80
XVIII.—Law-Abiding Australia: Lawless America 84
XIX.—"A Little Knowledge is a Dangerous Thing" 88
XX.—A Bad Carver Helps Nobody Well . . 91

XXI.—Bayley's at last Finds a Rival . . .	97
XXII.—" Swear not at all "	102
XXIII.—On 'Jumpers' and their Wicked Ways	105
XXIV.—The Government and the Water Question	108
XXV.—Siege of Londonderry. Huxley's Defence	113
XXVI.—Prospecting again Rewarded . . .	116
XXVII.—Western Australia's Chief Need: Population	120
XXVIII.—Advice Gratis is apt to be Worthless .	125
XXIX.—Declined with thanks . . .	130
XXX.—Ex Uno : Disce Omnes	134
XXXI.—An Advisory Syndicate . . .	138
XXXII.—The Command of the Sea . . .	142
XXXIII.—" Better to bear the ills we have, than to fly to others that we know not of .	147
XXXIV.—A Product of Joint Stock Enterprise : The Promoter	152
XXXV.—" Sun "-Light on West Australia . .	156
XXXVI.—Audi Alteram Partem	162
XXXVII.—A Vain Regret	166

I.—CONCERNING OUR OBJECTS.

This journal makes its appearance with the one main object of promoting the interests of Western Australia. In our opinion this can be best accomplished by making known as widely as possible the immense mineral wealth of the Colony. There are at present three great obstacles to her progress. The first is unalterable—her vast size. The second, the scantiness of her population, is being slowly removed. The third can readily be surmounted if confidence in her great mineral resources is once inspired. We refer to her lack of capital. When capital flows into Western Australia, population will follow. Her huge area of a million and sixty thousand square miles will cease to be a drawback, and will furnish a noble field for engineering triumphs. Money will cure the ills from which she suffers, and for this money she can offer ample security. To make known the riches of the unrivalled gold fields of this colony, to record what has been done, and to point out what can be done, will probably best attain the end we have in view.

The West Australian Review is designed to record, week by week, the latest and most trustworthy reports from the gold mines and alluvial diggings throughout the colony. It will also deal with the search after other metals, such as silver, tin, copper, &c. Diamonds have been found on the Nullagine, and leases have been granted by the Government to dig for them. Any success in this direction will have due attention. The colony possesses both coal and iron, and full accounts of the workings will be furnished.

It has been suggested that the pearl fisheries on the north-west coast come within the scope of this paper, and the strong interest that is felt in this subject will be our reason for devoting space to the concerns of this industry. Pearls, of course, occupy a solitary place in the great economy of nature, and as they are always associated with gold and other gems, it is only right to include them in a paper dealing with the most valuable products of the earth.

The ungathered wealth of Western Australia is so stupendous that such facts and figures as can be set down in these columns will give but a faint idea of her mighty possibilities. If however the light can be let in through such a chink as *The West Australian Review* proposes to furnish, its object will be gained; for when once the immense mineral stores of the colony are made known to the world, brains and skill will not be wanting to turn it into minted sovereigns.

II.—CONCERNING DIFFICULTIES AND DANGERS.

THE first number of our paper has been before the public for seven days. As we read it with critical eyes, the thought occurs that it is just possible that our objects may be misconstrued. This is the common fate of journals such as we have initiated. Once and for all then let us declare our intentions and motives. We seek nothing but the welfare of Western Australia. That giant colony, crippled in its birth by mismanagement; driven to such desperation as to accept such vile outcast scum of the earth as is ever held between the decks of a convict ship; yes! and thankful at the time for even that miserable means of assistance. None more forlorn than the "Cinderella of the South." But Western Australia, sneered at by Dampier, unvisited by Cook, has turned out to be pregnant. Pregnant with Gold! No richer reefs have gladdened men's eyes than lie untouched in that vast territory. It has been said that a hopeless region existed east of the 121st meridian of longitude and south of the 20th parallel of latitude. Nonsense, we answer; for that very virgin territory is full of that which makes men rich. Gold is there in enormous quantities, and if that be so, what fear can there be for the "Coming Colony"? If we can show this to be the case, as we contend we can, our main object is fulfilled. Money can buy the highest quality of brains.

and such engineers as bridged the Forth, or tunnelled the Severn, will not be wanting if gold is there. But just as of old—and always—men have been led to cast scruples to the winds when money is at stake, so, as is natural, men are trading on the tidings of expectant wealth, and Lilliputian John Laws take a glance at a piece of ground, acquire the claim from the Western Australian Government, and start to business on the Stock Exchange. In fact they, in plain terms, want to " boom " Western Australia, with a very obvious object in view. Now " booming " has well-nigh destroyed Victoria, and weakened Australian securities generally in an alarming degree.

We have good grounds for asserting that several gold mining companies are being prepared for the British investor. We sincerely hope that special caution will be exercised and every prospectus submitted to closest scrutiny. It is in the interests of the colony that we speak. A few bogus concerns forced on the market would mean something not unlike ruin to Western Australia. Yet nothing but capital and a population which surely follows will open up her vast mineral resources. The English public know little or nothing of this distant land. Still they have the testimony of such explorers as Sir John Forrest, Eyre, Giles, Warburton, and Messrs. Gregory. Nature has put such a *veto* against her advancement that nothing but the utmost resources of science will enable her mineral wealth to be developed. Water famine in many districts will jealously guard her golden stores. We speak not on our own authority, although we know something by experience of the dreary wastes which lie between Cambridge Gulf and Albany. But listen to Eyre, who with his faithful servant Baxter, two natives, and the boy Wylie, started in January, 1841, along the weary twelve months' trip from Adelaide to Perth. "No water, no water!" is the constant cry. After an interval of some thirty years, through the weary wilderness went John Forrest. Thus runs his journal, "This is the third day without a drop of water for the horses, which are in a frightful state." And again, "The land from Eucla to the head of the bight is entirely destitute of water." Nevertheless these starving, thirsty explorers have achieved their grand object. They have encountered the difficulties and the dangers, and told the gold miner what he had to expect.

Now the point we have in view is this. We know Western Australia to be anything but a "*land flowing with milk and honey:*" from the time that Dampier stigmatised the place as the most miserable spot on the globe, right up to the present day the world have had their eyes pretty well opened regarding the colony's drawbacks. No one would attempt to deny them with any show of reason. Nevertheless, now that it has been proved to be probably more full of gold than any other place on earth, it attracts the eye of the promoter of companies. The latest rush was in the Coolgardie direction, and leases have been taken up in this quarter by men who are utterly ignorant of the science of mining or mineralogy. To take up a claim and to write a prospectus is one thing; but to find gold and to make it pay is another. As we have stated, nature appears in an exceptionally antagonistic form in Western Australia; and skilled men only can decide on the merits of a gold claim. We have no desire to make enemies: quite the contrary. If in speaking the plain truth, however, regarding certain matters we incur dislike, we care not. We think it would be a grievous thing if this great golden colony should suffer at the hands of a few adventurers who have nothing to lose and everything to gain, by foisting worthless gold mines on the British public.

III.—WESTRALIA'S MINERALS: A RETROSPECT.

Down the centuries has come a faint echo declaring *Terra Incognita* or *Terra Australis*, to have been known as *Terra Aurifera*—that is a Gold-bearing Land. Uncertainty and doubt, however, surround all questions of early Australian discovery, both as regards the country itself, and its products. It is therefore impossible to state positively whether a Hollander, a Portugese, a Frenchman, or a Spaniard first set foot on the continent of Australia. The navigator who first landed on these desolate shores was almost certainly driven there against his will by adverse winds; and the coast upon which he landed must have been Western Australia, which lay nearest Africa and the Indies, in the direct track of weather driven vessels. Whether any of these fifteenth or sixteenth century mariners really discovered gold is extremely doubtful. Webbe, who accompanied William Dampier on his memorable voyage to the southern hemisphere, claimed to have come upon a territory of surpassing richness in both gold and silver. He even essayed to organise an expedition, and to raise capital for the purpose, but he failed in the attempt. Had he succeeded in his object, and had the diggings proved productive, Western Australia might have had a very different history. "Island of Gold," "Land of Gold," "Terra Aurifera," "Provincia

Aurifera," all these titles show the bent of the early navigators' and cartographers' minds. But in those days the alchemists were expecting to discover the Philosopher's Stone, which would have saved the trouble of prospecting and mining. People were more credulous at that time. They liked to have their spirits raised by tales of buried treasures of all kinds, nor did they even disdain to seek for a pot of gold where the end of a rainbow touches the earth. Transmutation of metals, however, has proved to be a fable; but we have over half a century of reliable West Australian history upon which we can take a firm stand, in connection with her mineral resources.

In 1840 lead and copper were discovered in the Champion Bay District, and the lodes were worked by English Companies. Then in 1846, the Messrs. Gregory discovered coal on the Irwin River, the field that is now in the hands of the Midland Railway Company.

In 1836, Mr. John Calvert wrote a book entitled "The Universal Distribution of the Metal Gold." In 1837, to further establish and illustrate his theory, he sailed to Sydney, and going up country discovered gold at Black Man's Swamp. Ten years elapsed—during which he had found gold in New Zealand and South Australia,—and in 1847, in command of the brigantine *Scout*, which he had purchased, Mr. Calvert cast anchor in Exmouth Gulf; and going inland discovered a rich tract of auriferous country on the Upper Murchison and the Upper Ashburton.

The first geologist employed by the Government was

Dr. Von Sommer, who made explorations between 1847 and 1851. Then Mr. A. C. Gregory and Mr. F. T. Gregory conducted expeditions, and published a geological map in 1860. Captain Roe, about the same time gives some valuable geological notes in his notes on his travels. Mr. H. Y. L. Brown made a geological examination of the colony in 1870-71, reporting on a strip of country some 50 miles wide, from the Murchison River to the south coast. Then in 1882 the late Mr. E. T. Hardman examined the Kimberley district; and it was his report of the same territory three years later which led to the establishment of the gold mining industry in Western Australia.

The "Cinderella of the South,"—as the colony has been called—was well stricken in years when the gold fever attacked her—at least she had attained the respectable age of 56.

Each of her colonial sisters had been seized with the epidemic in turn. First New South Wales, then Victoria; then South Australia (at Echunga); New South Wales had another attack at Snowy River; Queensland, at Gympie; New Zealand, Tasmania, and the Northern Territory of South Australia were all victims in turn. Lastly came Western Australia, and, judging from appearances, her ailment promises to become chronic, for truly her gold fields are so vast in extent, and so rich in the precious metal, as to be practically inexhaustible.

Mr. A. F. Calvert has made three explorations through the North West District, having started from London in April, 1890, and organised an expedition at his own expense. In April, 1891, he was engaged by the General Exploration Company, of London, to make further investigations in the same line of country, and in December, 1892, on the formation of the British Australian Exploration Company, he made a third journey on their behalf. He has also visited every sea port from Cambridge Gulf to King George's Sound, and made trips inland of various duration and with various objects in view.

Mr. John Calvert has been already referred to. He was and is a thoroughly practical miner, as well as a scientific geologist; and among the theories which he formulated from time to time in the forties, was one which had special application to Western Australia. He contended that gold would be found in parallels running across Australia, and that the western parallel would be the richest. Mr. A. F. Calvert was his pupil for many years, and has endeavoured to follow up some of his teacher's early investigations of half a century ago.

The great auriferous wealth of the western parallel has been abundantly proved. A belt of gold-bearing country extends from Phillip's River in the south up through the Yilgarn, Murchison, Gascoyne, and Ashburton Gold field. Then there seems to be a parallel further to the east, extending from Dundas Hills in the south, to Ularring and Kimberley Range, then passing the heads of the Murchison and Ashburton Rivers, and possibly reaching to Marble Bar and Nullagine, where the belt may possibly be intersected by another, which running east and west cuts it at right angles. This latter assumption is not put forward as an ascertained fact, but merely as a possible suggestion as to the general run of the gold reefs.

It is impossible to exaggerate the magnificent outlook on these vast tracts of auriferous territory. With the progress of exploration and discovery, new sources of wealth are appearing, and immense openings are revealing themselves for the employment of capital and labour.

Many of the alluvial deposits have already yielded large returns without the use of machinery. These cannot however be reasonably expected to last. The future prosperity and permanency of West Australian gold fields lie in the working of her great quartz-reefs. To efficiently do this demands enterprise on a large scale, backed by capital and a scientific skill. Then will the element of chance be reduced to a minimum, and gold mining be conducted on a basis of systematic calculation, like any other branch of industry.

Distance, drought and scarcity of timber, from which some districts suffer, are difficulties of nature which, however can be largely overcome by science ; and the vast mineral wealth to be secured, will amply justify the employment of the best means known to man.

IV.—EARLY GOLD DISCOVERY.

In the early days of the colonization of New South Wales, a convict named Smith, anxious to break the monotony of prison treatment, and perhaps hoping to shake the manacles off his toil-worn limbs, made a statement to the effect that he had discovered a veritable gold mine. He offered to reveal its locality on certain conditions, and on being called upon to show his treasure find, after much coaxing, he at last pointed to a little sand run in Sydney Cove towards the "Heads." For a few feet around the spot there were evidences of some brass filings having been scattered and mixed with the sand for a few inches down. The fraud was immediately detected, and the poor wretch had to pay a heavy price for the few days relaxation he had obtained, for he was ordered the lash and a reduction of his scanty rations.

After this occurrence no more was heard about gold until Mr. John Calvert—who had already issued a pamphlet, in which he had claimed that gold was universally and generally distributed in nearly every part of the world—voyaged to Australia for the express object of establishing his theory, by practically extracting the precious metal from its various ores and matrices. In 1837, he landed at Sydney, and instead of following the example of the convict in looking for gold in the sandstone around Sydney, he boldly struck out for the ranges to the west, and was not long in attaining his object.

All the tributaries of the Macquarie River, that he investigated, he found to be auriferous; but at Black Man's Swamp near the Canobolas, he discovered a most interesting and very strong system of gold reefs. A portion of the outcrop consisted of earthy oxide of iron, richly bespangled with fine native gold gave very good results by simply crushing, with the assistance of the blacks; and by rough washing the ironstone an appreciable amount of gold was obtained. Some years afterwards, during the reign of "Billy Wentworth" in those parts, this same ironstone was used in the construction of a bridge, he being a disbeliever in the existence of gold at that time. This the Turon gold-diggers in 1852 got scent of, and in spite of "Billy Wentworth's" remonstrances, the whole of the bridge was demolished in a few days, the rich ironstone pulverised, and its shiny particles turned into bullion.

In 1838, Mr. John Calvert sailed to New Zealand, making a short stay there, sufficiently long however to establish the fact, of his declaration as to the universal distribution of the metal, gold. He then returned to Sydney, *en route* for England, arriving in London in 1840. Several works thereafter issued from his pen, and in 1843 he sailed for the Southern Continent in the *Augustus* (Captain Hart), in company with his friend, George French Angus. He spent some time in South Australia, after which he continued his journey to Sydney and gathered a large amount of bullion, some of which he sold to a Mr. Cohen, jeweller in George Street, Sydney, who exhibited it in his shop window, to which fact many old colonists now living can testify.

The following is an extract of a letter that appeared in the *Sydney Star* of September 5th, 1890 :—

"Mr. Joseph Levy, of Balmain, writes confirming the assertion made in the interview that Mr. John Calvert was first to discover gold in these colonies, and stating that he (Mr. Levy) remembered seeing as a boy the first specimens displayed in a shop in George Street."

It is of interest to note that in 1844 Mr. Calvert sent home to Sir Roderick Murchison a letter stating how successful he had been in verifying the statements he had put forward in his works, more especially in "The universal distribution of the metal Gold," and that now, by actual survey and travel, he had established the fact that Australia had many rich veins of gold associated with quartz and other minerals, and also that over vast tracts of country, gold might be obtained by washing the alluvial and river drifts. He also forwarded to Sir Roderick a small piece of veritable gold quartz.

After Mr. Calvert had investigated the mineral districts of South Australia and the North West, he concluded from their geological formation that the gold ores of the eastern and western parallels were richer. Accordingly he proceeded to Sydney, and attempted to induce the Government to take the matter up, but without success.

The leading officials in those days failed to perceive the expediency of fostering the mining industry. The

Governor, the Colonial Secretary, and the Surveyor-General, all treated the discovery as a matter of very little consequence. The feeling in official circles may be gathered from a letter written on the subject to Mr. Calvert by Sir Thomas Mitchell, in which he said: "We are a pastoral and agricultural community and do not desire inducements held out for people to dig holes for our sheep and cattle to tumble into."

Having brought away numerous specimens, Calvert divulged his knowledge to several scientists of the day, including the Rev. W. B. Clarke, who afterwards wrote a book re-enunciating Calvert's theory of gold in parallels under the thin disguise of latitude and longitude.

With the accumulation of several years gold digging, in 1847, Mr. Calvert bought a brigantine of 240 tons. It was called the *Scout*; and was well manned and equipped. In this vessel he first visited Port Macquarie, Van Diemen's Land, to search the mountains there for gold, which he found. Subsequently, in the same year, he sailed for Exmouth Gulf, Western Australia.

The shadowy tales of old voyagers who had been driven by adverse winds on the desolate shores of Western Australia, gave hints of their having found gold in these wild regions. The old map-makers of the sixteenth century rang the changes between *aurifera* and *incognita* in naming *Terra Australis* in their atlases; and moreover, Mr. Calvert had formulated a theory that gold would be found in parallels running across Australia, and that the Western parallel would be the richest. Recent discoveries are every day adding strength and confirmation to this doctrine. The *Scout* cast anchor in Exmouth Gulf, when he disembarked his equipment, and unloaded his horses; and after following up the Ashburton for a considerable distance, he left the valley, and ascended the range dividing the waters of the upper Ashburton and upper Murchison. Here he found occasional outcrops of gold quartz, and he came upon a quartz blow, which he considered the richest surface out-crop of gold quartz he had ever seen.

Early in 1849 Mr. Calvert was again in London, where he endeavoured to float a company to work the gold-mines of Australia, but met with little encouragement. Had he been successful in floating this company, it was his intention to proceed direct to the Murchison, West Australia, but having failed in his attempt he made up his mind to return to his first discovery. He therefore started again for Australia in the *Mount Stewart Elphinstone*, and determined to start working for himself, taking with him various gold-saving appliances. He landed at Adelaide and washed gold in South Australia, a few of the leading men following him by invitation into the field, which formed subject matter for the Adelaide papers of that date. Moreover a full page engraving was given in one of the illustrated papers of January, 1850, entitled "The run for gold," and some of the gold-saving machines he had brought out from England were depicted in that illustration.

Before the end of 1850 he had accumulated considerable gold to the west of the Blue Mountains; but inasmuch as he employed white as well as black labour, his doings were soon the talk of the little town of Bathurst. About this time a blacksmith named Hargreaves, who had returned from California, as a penniless and unsuccessful digger, arrived in the neighbourhood and sought to reinstate himself as a blacksmith in the town of Bathurst. Mrs. Lister, who kept a roadside inn, gave him shelter, and at her drinking bar Hargreaves met Toms, who had been employed by Mr. Calvert, and had seen him wash gold in Summer Hill Creek. When Hargreaves heard the story from young Lister and Toms, an idea struck him that he might better his fortunes and create a sensation by washing gold in a new locality. He therefore bargained with Toms and Lister to show him the spot, and promised them half of any reward or advantage that might be obtained. The bargain was struck, and the next day a Californian tin dish was made to Hargreaves' pattern. Toms and Lister fulfilled their part of the contract by taking him to the exact spot that they had seen Mr. Calvert wash gold. They were not aware at the time that other parts of the Creek would have given gold. It is needless to recount the subsequent story which has been often told. Hargreaves made a claim upon the Government, which they handsomely responded to; but he was not honest enough to keep faith with his partners — Toms and Lister. In consequence of this, they for years harassed the Government with their claims, denouncing Hargreaves as an imposter. Indeed, it was not until the Government had referred to Mr. John Calvert, who was on a visit to Sydney in 1890, and supported the Toms and

Lister story, that they seriously looked into the matter. A committee was appointed by the Government, who unhesitatingly deprived Hargreaves of all his assumed honours, and for ever set aside his claim as the discoverer of gold in Australia.

The Rev. W. B. Clarke and Hargreaves had both made a claim upon the Government to reward them for the parts they had played in connection with the discovery of gold. At the time the matter was under consideration Mr. Calvert had returned to England, and not being on the spot he did not make any counter-claim, nor did he in any way dispute their pretentions.

He was consequently at a loss to understand the reason for the severe attacks made upon him over the signature of Hargreaves, and the several leading articles which appeared in the *Sydney Morning Herald*, emanating from the pen of the Rev. W. B. Clarke. They both knew what a serious opponent he would be, should he come to the front, hence, the scurrilous attacks anticipating his prior claims in that field of discovery. Mr. Calvert treated their vituperation with contempt, as he felt their design was too transparent to deceive anyone concerned.

On Mr. Calvert's return to England he was rather astonished to find that Sir Roderick Murchison had laid claim to discovery of gold in Australia. He saw, however, that his hypothesis was unsound, inasmuch as he had ignored the silurian rocks of North Wales, which Mr. Calvert knew from former investigations were auriferous. He, therefore, resolved to challenge him upon the subject, and for that purpose he read several papers upon gold in Australia and gold in Great Britain.

The best defence Sir Roderick could make was that "he did not expect to find gold in our home rocks." The following extract is from a report of a paper read at the Hull meeting of the British Association in 1853 :—

"Mr. Calvert went on to say, 'Although you have written much to prove the identity of the Welsh rocks with those of the Ural, still you have been silent as to their being auriferous.' He concluded his speech by asserting that the Welsh rocks were extensively auriferous, and offered to meet Sir Roderick and his friends on the Welsh mountains, where he would point out rich veins of quartz."

The challenge was duly accepted. The parties met at Dolgelly, and Mr. Calvert took them to Clogau, broke gold from the rocks, and turned the tables on his scientific antagonist.

Mr. Calvert had called attention to the vast mineral wealth of Western Australia in his paper at the British Association meeting of 1853. This was chiefly founded on the observations he had made during his expedition to the Upper Murchison in 1847, and also in the second edition of his work entitled "The Gold Rocks," where it was even more strongly dealt with, and a copy of which he had presented to Sir Roderick. Nevertheless, in 1844 Sir Roderick promulgates one of his greatest blunders upon the subject of gold, which will for ever dispose of his authority as a gold expert.

In his Presidential Address to the Royal Geographical

Society, in May, 1844, which can be found in the Journal, page 100, Sir Roderick Impey Murchison, after pointing out the similarity of the rocks forming the great chain running down the eastern side of Australia, and re-continuing into Tasmania, to those of the Ural mountains, speaks as follows: " But it " (referring to the Australian chain) differs from the Ural and many other meridian chains in having as yet offered no trace of gold or auriferous veins."

Again, in 1864, as may be seen in the Proceedings of The Geological Society (vol. viii., 1864, page 32), a man named Hargreaves read a paper on the non-auriferous character of the rocks of Western Australia. Sir Roderick occupied the chair as president. Here is the report of his remarks :—

"The President, in expressing the customary vote of thanks to the author for the paper, said, Mr. Hargreaves was the first practical explorer of gold mines in Australia. He had been sent out by Government to see if Western Australia would prove auriferous. He had stated what certainly was a fact, that he (Sir R. I. Murchison) never had the remotest idea of suggesting that Western Australia would prove auriferous on the contrary; he knew very well that from what had been previously said of the structure of those rocks, and from the fossils and organic remains which had been brought before them by Mr. Frank Gregory, who had explored the country, that there were none of those ancient slaty rocks in the regions examined with quartz veins in them in which gold could be discovered."

From the first quotation it seems clear that Sir Roderick merely drew attention to a similarity between the rocks of Eastern Australia and certain other gold-bearing rocks in other parts of the world; and in the second he gives as his opinion that gold would not be found at all in Western Australia. Sir Roderick's mistake did much to retard the development of the gold fields of Western Australia.

Mr. John Calvert was deeply engaged in the perfecting of his decomposing process; and had no leisure to devote to Western Australia. From time to time, however, he made allusion to the rich outcrops of gold quartz that he had seen in the Murchison, and it is just possible that one of his finds, which has been called the Treasure reef, was despoiled by Palmer and his party in 1891, shortly after the diggers rushed to that locality. In a cutting from a West Australian paper of that date a tent full of rich gold quartz is described, and the appearance of the reef is similar to what Mr. Calvert remembered of it. One particular statement made by Mr. Calvert is contained in a letter to the *Times* of December 28th, 1887, of which the following is an extract :—

"Some extraordinary and glorious evidences of packing occur in the Western ranges of Tasmania, also New Zealand and New Guinea, but in Western Australia I found the most wonderful evidence of the surrounding country having been robbed to the benefit of a small area of about 50 yards, the gold being packed against a stop which had arrested it during its charge while in solution. No bunch of gold I have ever seen in North or South America, or in any other part of the world, approaches in richness or value to this outcrop."

This letter was, no doubt, the means of calling attention to the then undeveloped rich gold fields of Western Australia. Mr. John Calvert was beseiged by letters, both from home and from the colonies, and all kinds of propositions were laid before him inviting him to locate the spot from memory. The discovery of the Murchison in 1891 was no doubt owing in a great measure to the sensation caused by the correspondence that ensued.

One local paper, the *Geraldton-Murchison Telegraph*, of January 13th, 1893, in an article, made the following allusion to Mr. Calvert:—

"Mr. John Calvert, now 80 years of age, was, and is still, a remarkable man. An enthusiastic student of the science of geology, his name has for sixty years past a prominent one in the scientific world. The geology of Australia, particularly of Western Australia, always possessed for him a special interest, and if we are not mistaken it was he, and not the eminent Sir Roderick Murchison, who prophesied such great things for this colony, and who indicated that North-West Australia would prove a fruitful field for the future gold-miner."

The Inquirer, of Perth, January 21st, 1893, said:—

"As regards the senior Mr. Calvert's wonderful reports and prophecies concerning the mineral riches of Western Australia, this at least may be said, that he was far more accurate in his observations than men like Hargreaves and other reputed authorities on gold mining, who affirmed that the precious metal would never be found in the colony in payable quantities."

IV.—CONCERNING OTHER MINERAL RESOURCES.

The ring of gold seems to silence the jingle of baser metals, just as the forest is hushed to stillness when the lion lifts up his mighty voice. Gold is another name for riches, power — indeed pretty nearly everything this world affords, except health and happiness. The gold fields of Western Australia are a heritage of vast import, and it is not to be denied that upon their skilful and successful working, combined with truthful representation, much of the colony's future prosperity depends.

We should be doing her an injustice, however, did we not refer to her other mineral treasures, which, even if gold had never been discovered, would deserve attention.

As we have before stated, this journal has no intention of 'booming' any particular mine or gold field, or promoting any individual special item. We desire to lay a plain statement of facts before our readers, unaffected by bias or private interest. Gold will of necessity claim the chief place; but it will not monopolise our paper to the exclusion of such important industries as are connected with tin, copper, coal, iron, lead, and other minerals. According to their merits, as we receive news of progress in these directions, they shall have due attention.

The discovery of one metal often leads to the discovery of another, and in working the ores with one main object in view, other secondary objects are often attained by the liberation of metals which lay in combination, and which scientifically treated, immensely enhance the profits, and lessen cost of production. In short we want to show that Western Australia is a great mineral country, and that when the eyes of the world are opened to this fact, her resources are bound to be developed. Her gold may be depended upon to give the impetus needed. It can open most locks, and solve most problems. Still, as we have stated, her mineral endowments are not confined to the precious metal.

Probably before gold was known at all, tin played a prominent part in shaping the destinies of mankind. Copper may be said to have been an equally important factor in the world's progress. The reason is not far to seek. Bronze was the forerunner of iron, and bronze is a blend of copper and tin. Prehistoric man had long fashioned stone into rude implements of agriculture and weapons of war; but what inroad could the blunt stone axe make upon the virgin forests of the world ? A metal was needed sufficiently hard to keep a keen edge. In all likelihood copper was tried first, but although more easily shaped than stone, it was too soft to be of practical value. At length, by some happy accident, a combination with tin was made, and found to produce a fairly hard metal, and thus was begun that great epoch of bygone time known as the " Bronze Age." From thenceforward man emerged from savagery and advanced towards civilization. Hard metal implied smelting, casting, &c., and gradually led up to hundreds of useful arts.

Then observe how tin affected commerce and navigation. Up to very recently there were only two parts of the world where it could be procured in large quantity, viz., Cornwall and the Malay Archipelago. This necessitated a sea-going trade in tin, and first tempted the Phœnicians past the Pillars of Hercules to brave the terrors of the Atlantic. Thus it may be said that the foundation of England's early commerce was tin. It was probably shipped from the old port of Richborough in the time of the Romans; but a trade in this metal was carried on long centuries before the Roman occupation of Britain.

The remains of a very old road, traversing England from Cornwall to the Isle of Thanet, still exists; and along this track the ancient Britons were wont to bring their ingots of metal to the port of shipment.

The value of gold is, of course, largely artificial, and owes its origin, not to its practical utility for industrial purposes, but to its comparative rarity, and its adoption as the money standard of the world. As a useful metal for making a sword, a plough, or a battle-axe, the modest penny would be more serviceable than the lordly sovereign. We will not dispute the rank and grandeur of gold however; for at its will all metals are melted and moulded to a thousand shapes. The iron glows and ascends the throne as king of useful metals, ploughing the seas in ships, spanning rivers in bridges, engirdling the earth in railways; and in flashing swords or thundering cannon, spreading devastation and conferring glory.

Tin is a vastly important metal, nevertheless, and the few preceding remarks have been introduced in order that it may be appreciated at its proper value as one of nature's greatest gifts to mankind. Again, curiously enough we find "Tin" used as a synonym for money—a sort of colloquial and slangy recognition of its importance. The same may be said of "Brass," however, so we will not venture to touch on verbal eccentricities.

V.—RELICS OF A SUNKEN WRECK.

A great reef off the coast of Edel's Land in Western Australia is known by the title of "Houtman's Abrolhos." The name is curious and rather enigmatical. The first word is Dutch, the second Portuguese. Frederick Houtman was the commercial chief of an expedition undertaken by the Dutch in 1595. Whether he ever saw Western Australia is uncertain. He probably found the money, and he seems to have assumed the title of "Captain-General." His name, however, is attached to the reef in question, although probably the honour of discovering the rocks has been falsely conferred upon him. So much then for the Dutch moiety of the appellation. The second half is, as we have stated, of Portuguese origin, and signifies "Keep your eyes open" It is not hard to imagine how this came about. We can well imagine the terror of the Portuguese captain if he happened to be on the look-out when he found his little ship, battered and tempest-tossed, heading on for the black rocks, veiled by the surges of the Indian Ocean. It was, indeed, a case of "Keep your eyes open" in that wild hand-gallop over those stormy seas. It may well be supposed that the captain wrote "Abrolhos" on his chart, and offered up a prayer of thankfulness for his escape. Some think the discoverer was Menezes in 1527, but it is not probable. Galvano, his historian, does not say so. Very soon after his voyage, however, the cartographers got to know of these rocks, for they are marked on their atlases. The word "Abrolhos," however, only appears on the chart of Pierre Desceliers in 1550. Desceliers was a priest, and they knew most things in those days.

Everything, however, has its use in the great economy of nature, and so it is with Houtman's Abrolhos. These rocks are the home of the seabirds, and the guano deposits are valuable. Mr. Broadhurst had the contract when Mr. A. F. Calvert was in Perth, and knowing the keen interest he took in early Australian history, he brought round to the hotel some silver coins which had been found by his men in the course of their excavations. Some of these were Spanish, and bore the superscription, "1616 Hispaniarum Rex." Evidently some Spanish navigator had come to grief, in spite of the warning of his rivals to "Keep your eyes open." Mr. William John Gordan has reproduced one of these coins on the cover of his book, "The Captain-General." What brought the Spaniard into that quarter at that date it is hard to say. With the commencement of the seventeenth century, they had practically resigned their dominion on the sea; and the down-trodden Netherlander was coming to the front. When Pedro Fernando de Qùiros died at Panama in 1614, the last great captain disappears from Spanish history. Britannia ruled the waves later on, and we held the power and glory of Spain pretty cheap when the "Invincible Armada" was blown off the waters,—not altogether by British cannon, however. "Give the Devil his due " is a phrase sometimes used, but we are not prone to have very kindly thoughts about King Henry VIII. Nevertheless, had it not been for that same monarch—brutal as he was—his daughter Elizabeth would have had less confidence when she reviewed her army and navy at Tilbury. Our naval supremacy is a matter of comparatively recent date.

But to return to Houtman's Abrolhos, Sir Malcolm Fraser lent the proprietor of this journal, a photographic presentment of some relics which have recently come to light by the guano workers.

Much as the shores of Australia were dreaded by the Dutch mariners by reason of the many shipwrecks which had occurred, the Dutch East India Company took pains to fill their coffers by means of maritime adventure. Their avarice was insatiable, and regarding their ways and means history may well be silent. "*De Mortuis nil nisi Bonum*," is a proverb of noble sentiment. A great poet, Shakespeare by name, scarcely echoes the Latin writer, when he exclaims, "The evil that men do lives after them." Still, let us content ourselves with the verdict of "Nil," regarding the Dutch East India Company. They remembered the names of their ships, but forgot those of their captains. They darkened the light of history by their concealment of records, and still they achieved success. No country has ever fought such a battle with nature as the Dutchman. To him we render the credit which it is impossible to deny.

The following is an extract from Mr. Calvert's recently published work on "The Discovery of Australia":

"Between the years 1720 and 1730, several Dutch vessels were lost on Houtman's Abrolhos when journeying from the East Indies. Among these were the *Zuysdorp* in 1711, and the *Zeewyk* in 1727. In 1840 an English commander, whose name is given as "Crawford Pako " (but no such name is so written in the Navy List of that date), found here various remains of shipwrecks, viz :—a brass gun, Dutch bottles, large buckles, and copper coins, dated between 1620 and 1700."

We do not happen to have at hand a Navy List of that date ; but would hazard a guess that "Parker" might be the name intended.

Now the relics above referred to, the photograph of which we have been permitted to inspect through the courtesy of Sir Malcolm Fraser, are described as "Relics from the Dutch vessel *Zeewyk*, wrecked on Houtman's Abrolhos, Western Australia, in the year 1727."

They consist of the following miscellaneous articles :

Three large and 24 small cannon balls ; 15 flagon-shaped bottles ; 10 square gin bottles ; one earthenware jar ; 14 rosary beads ; nine lead sinkers ; 22 pipes and stems ; five copper fish hooks ; five knives ; six pieces of lock flint ; seven brass buttons ; five lead weights ; 16 pistol bullets ; two kettles ; one brass tap ; one pot ; one copper vessel, with cover for padlocking ; one leaden ink-pot ; one wine glass ; two colored tumblers ; two pieces of ordnance ; one silver coin ; three copper coins ;—and many sundry odds and ends, including a small piece of copper marked "Zeeland," and two remains of block sheaves. These are all lying in the Museum at Perth,

Western Australia; and we shall hope to have a more definite description from some competent judge, who can speak as to the nationality and the period they represent. Meantime we fail to see how—upon the evidence before us—the relics are specially connected with the *Zeewyk*. Many other vessels went to pieces on those rocks, as, for instance, the *Zuysdorp* in 1711 and the *Batavia* in 1629. In fact the Dutch East Indiamen were constantly coming to grief. They carried enormous crews, besides numerous passengers, and in case of accident they were totally unprovided for. Thevenot's account of the last-named disaster is painfully graphic. On the night of the 4th of June, 1629, the ship struck, and its immense freight managed to get upon the rocks. At daylight an island nine miles off was sighted, which the passengers and crew managed by many painful journeys to reach ; but could find no fresh water. Francis Pelsart, the captain, and a few of the sailors then sailed for the mainland, and finding it as barren as the rocky islet they had left, determined to make for Batavia. This they reached, and Pelsart, in the yacht *Saardam*, returned to rescue any of the shipwrecked survivors. On his return he discovered that they had actually found water ; but the supercargo Cornelis had formed a dastardly plot to seize the *Saardam* and go on a pirating expedition. He and his conspirators had actually massacred 125 of the people—men, women and children—and came off in two boats with the view of murdering their rescuers. Their conspiracy was happily detected, and many were hanged. Two had possibly a worse fate, for they were put ashore on the mainland, and probably died of starvation. Fifteen years afterwards we read in Tasman's 'Book of Despatches' that he was instructed to endeavour to fish up a chest of rix dollars lost in the *Batavia's* wreck, and to look out for Pelsart's marooned mutineers, to see if they had found out anything which might be of service to the Company.

Then again, Spanish caravels, Portuguese and French vessels must have been shattered on the terrible reefs. We should like to know, moreover, something of the coins found. Were they Dutch? And lastly, were the Dutch likely to use rosary beads? It is much to be desired that all such relics obtained should find their way into the Government museum; for it is impossible to assert that there may not be yet found some precious memorials of the past, which may help to clear up much of the mystery which surrounds the early history of Western Australia. The finders of such relics should be amply rewarded when they surrender them to the authorities. Their intrinsic value may be small; but they may be of inestimable worth in their relations to the problem which has not yet been solved as to the First Discoverers of Australia.

VI.—A PLEA FOR SPECIMENS AT THE IMPERIAL INSTITUTE.

"Western Australia and its Welfare." These words sum up the aim and objects of this journal. Having seen for ourselves her wondrous mineral wealth, her splendid possibilities, it was our desire and ambition to make these matters known in England, and by publishing a colonial journal in London, to form a connecting tie between the old country and the new. The results of all such efforts, whether in the religious, social, political or commercial world, show themselves very slowly as a rule, and frequently remain invisible. Naturally we have often asked ourselves the question, *Cui bono?* Have we really done any solid and lasting good for the colony to which we are devoted? At length —through the clouds of indifference, neglect, and perhaps jealousy, which have at times darkened our horizon— there bursts a joyous gleam of encouragement.

In our first issue, some four months ago, we strongly condemned the apathy of the authorities in Perth, who allowed their grand and growing colony to be represented (or rather misrepresented) at the Imperial Institute in South Kensington, by "a beggarly account of empty boxes, thinly scattered, to make up a show." We suggested that it would be better either to shut up the show altogether, or send to the care of Sir Malcolm Fraser, something worth exhibiting, and representative of the "Coming Colony." "Victoria," we remarked in the same issue, "has a dazzling display of *models* of big nuggets won from the earth, ever so many years ago. Let this be capped by some wise purchases of the *real metal* and rich quartz, which would necessitate insurance and the constant attendance of a policeman to guard the treasure, which latter precaution would be an invaluable standing advertisement at a nominal cost."

It was depressing in the extreme to see the boundless resources of the Land of the Black Swan thus ignored and forgotten in this great national representative Colonial Temple; and the proprietor of this journal endeavoured in some slight degree to supplement deficiencies from his private collection. The gold specimens he sent, however, only seemed to make the deficiency more obvious, for nothing short of a national effort will adequately represent national products.

It is, however, most encouraging to learn that our suggestions have been taken up by the Government and the Press of Western Australia, with the result that strenuous exertions are being made to furnish an exhibit which will redound to the credit of this rising mineral colony. The work of making such a collection has been entrusted to the Museum authorities at Perth, who have sent circulars round the colony asking aid in the way of suggestions, and seeking for objects of special colonial interest. From both private individuals, and through editorial channels in the Press, a ready response has been given.

One paper, *The Geraldton-Murchison Telegraph*, gives us credit for having initiated this most desirable movement. After quoting our remarks in connection with the purchase of specimens, &c., already referred to, and commending our suggestions, our contemporary goes on to say: "Especially should it be made clear to the Old World public, that whereas some rivals, who shall not be named, are in certain mineral respects more or less rapidly becoming extinct volcanoes, Western Australian riches are still comparatively untouched, and the Coming Colony, with only 60,000 folk to share it, has mineral wealth enough for the whole world."

The chief newspaper organ in the colony, *The West Australian*, devotes a leading article to the same question, and urges its importance upon the Government in the following practical words:—

"For a few hundred pounds the Curator of the Museum can get together a very salient collection of gold and other specimens. But the Government might do more than this—they might determine to purchase the next instalment of gold and specimens which arrive from Bayley's claim, and keep them on view at the Institute and elsewhere for some months. This might cost £10,000 or more, the interest on which they would of course lose for the period during which the specimens and bullion were on view, but this loss of interest would be far more than made up by the influx of wealth into Western Australia which would certainly result. It would, in fact, be an investment of the best possible character. The gold could not run away unless it were stolen, which is not likely, and thousands would flock to see the precious metal in the form in which it has recently been shown to admiring crowds in Melbourne."

We are indeed grateful for these tokens of appreciation. Imitation is said to be the sincerest form of flattery, and the imitation of our sentiments, or the adoption of our views, we apprehend, is so sincere as to deserve a better name than flattery. We look forward eagerly to the comsummation of our hopes in the direction of the Imperial Institute, and we hope to see a day, in the near future, when the British public will crowd into the West Australian section of the Imperial Institute, and gaze with admiration on a noble collection of quartz and nuggets fresh from mother earth, solid, silent, and undoubted witnesses of the greatest gold fields in the world.

VII.—CONCERNING THE HOMESTEADS ACT.

With the view of giving the widest publicity in our power to the generous provisions of the "Homesteads Act, 1893," we have devoted four pages of our paper, for the past three weeks, to the full text of Sir John Forrest's wise and liberal measure. It gives the proprietor of *The Register* the utmost satisfaction to thus give effect to his keen and absorbing interest in the welfare of Western Australia.

Now that the Act has become law, after somewhat prolonged discussion, our first feeling is one of thankfulness that "all is over." That feeling, which, in a much more concentrated form, has lifted a load from many a manly heart, when the announcement came to his anxious ear that the population of the world had been increased through his instrumentality. To carry out the parallel a little farther, the next feeling is one of gratitude. And now the analogy ceases, for the cordial thanks and congratulations of the whole Colony—nay, of the countless multitudes outside the Colony who may take advantage of the Act—are due to the parent of this great and comprehensive Land Act—Sir John Forrest.

Well might he say with Horace, "*Exegi monumentum œre perennius.*" The Latin poet was alluding to his own works—his odes, his epistles, aud his satires—and like many other poets he was a vain, conceited man,—which no doubt, in a sense, he had every right to be. This consummation of the Premier's strenuous and long-sustained efforts is indeed a monument more lasting than brass, and loftier than the regal summits of the pyramids. Had he never done anything else for Western Australia; had his whole life not been devoted to her interests; he would have earned her lasting gratitude and inscribed his name indelibly on her archives by the inception and carrying through of this most excellent measure.

Festina lente has ever been the motto of the Westralians, and indeed they have sometimes carried the principle of caution too far. It is all very well to "hurry slowly," but there is a degree of slowness at which motion seems to cease. A rash country is no doubt a bad country; but a stagnant country is worse. The former at least lives, even if it lives too freely; the latter dies. On the whole, Western Australia may be said to have adopted a medium course. She had of necessity to "go slow." She was like an immense ocean steamer with neither horse-power nor sails sufficient to give her speed. Still she has not drifted. She has managed in times past to keep off a lee shore, with the aid of a storm try-sail.

Canada, the United States, South America, and South Africa have been holding out attractive offers to emigrants, and it was high time the "Coming Colony" followed their example. She can well afford to be liberal, with nearly seven hundred millions of acres at her command.

Our journal is, doubtless, devoted largely to mining,

as its name implies; but everything which concerns Western Australia—directly or indirectly—has a welcome place in our columns. We cannot but feel assured that the "Homesteads Act" will attract emigrants to the colony, when the benefits offered by the Act itself, and the capabilities of the country, are made widely known. We will not now speak of her mining possibilities, which are every day becoming more apparent. But when intending settlers are made aware that the Colony possesses one of the most salubrious climates in the world; that the mortality since its occupation has not averaged $1\frac{1}{4}$ per cent.; that it is subjected to no extremes of heat or cold; that the hills and valleys and grassy plains are unexampled fields for the energies of the agricultural or pastoral farmer; and *that poverty for the industrious is impossible;* then may we expect to see the full fruition of the Homesteads Act.

Without having the precise figures before us, we are unable to make a comparison of the fees payable by free selectors. But we may say with confidence that they are much lower than those of the United States of America, where, after all, the costs of "entering," "proving up," &c., are comparatively small. In the Great Republic certain abuses of the system have, doubtless, crept in. We know of men, now living in Colorado, who have taken up hundreds of claims on the "dummy" plan. A friend of the writer's was once offered to be placed in free possession of 160 acres of land—that is, all preliminary expenses, &c., to be paid—on condition of his allowing his name to be used, and the land-operator, who was to pay all, was merely to have for his share *all the timber on the land*. It would have been a bad bargain, for the timber was the only thing of any value on the claim in question, which was on a slope of the Rocky Mountains. Moreover, for making a false declaration, the bogus free selector rendered himself liable to a sojourn in a State prison. The offer was declined, as it happened, but many new comers to the States are induced to take up land in this way for the benefit of a few shrewd and unscrupulous American capitalists, who thereby acquire thousands of acres. It has been said that "a coach and four can be driven through an Act of Parliament." This is extremely figurative, but bears a true enough interpretation. Laws cannot be framed perfectly so as to cover all contingencies, and the best are liable to be undermined by unprincipled men.

ALBERT F. CALVERT AT THE ROYAL COLONIAL INSTITUTE.

It is gratifying to find that the progress of Western Australia is becoming a subject of absorbing interest among all classes of society in the United Kingdom. Capitalists, railway contractors, engineers, mining experts, miners, farmers, artisans and labourers, are being attracted to this colony, whose mineral resources, agricultural and pastoral capabilities have more and more displayed themselves to the view of the civilized world. If our humble efforts in these columns have in some measure contributed to this end, our labours will not have been in vain. " Western Australia and its Welfare " has been our watchword, and it has been from the first our aim and object to present the public each week with a clear and consistent account of her steady advance and development.

Many of our readers are familiar with that august body known as "The Royal Colonial Institute," who have premises in Northumberland Avenue, London. For the enlightenment of those who are not acquainted with its foundation and objects, a few words of explanation may be needful. The Institute was founded in 1868; and afterwards, in 1882, incorporated by Royal Charter. H.R.H. the Prince of Wales is President, and the list of Vice-Presidents includes some of the most distinguished names in England, as, for instance, H.R.H.

Prince Christian, the Duke of Argyle, the Marquis of Dufferin, the Marquis of Lorne, the Earl of Dunraven, the Earl of Rosebery, Viscount Monck, Lord Brassey, and others. "United Empire" is the motto of the Institute, and its purpose is to provide a place of meeting for all gentlemen connected with the Colonies and India, and likewise for those who take an interest in Colonial and Indian affairs. To establish a reading room and library, where recent and reliable information on Colonial and Indian subjects may be obtained; and also a Museum for the exhibition of Colonial and Indian productions. To facilitate the interchange of experiences amongst persons represented or interested in the various British dependencies, and to furnish opportunities for reading of papers and holding discussions. Likewise, to undertake scientific, literary, and statistical investigations in connection with the above subjects. In short, the design and purpose of the Institute is to extend knowledge respecting the various portions of the British Empire, and to promote the cause of its permanent unity.

In the Report of Proceedings for 1892-93, we find that at the first ordinary meeting of the Institute Sir Malcolm Fraser read a paper on "The Present Condition and Prospects of Western Australia." Lord Brassey, who is a large holder of land in the Colony, presided, and with true hereditary instinct strongly advocated the construction of railways. We need hardly say that the Agent-General's interesting and exhaustive paper was cordially received and highly commended, emanating as it did from a distinguished member of the Government, with twenty-two years experience of Western Australia.

On Wednesday last, the 24th of January, Mr. Albert Calvert, F.R.G.S., the founder and proprietor of this journal, read a paper before the Fellows of the Royal Colonial Institute on "Western Australia and its Goldfields." After shortly alluding to her scantiness of population, her lack of capital, and her water difficulty, he gave a rapid sketch of the first discovery of gold in 1847 by Mr. John Calvert, and referred to his theory of gold being found in parallels across Australia, the most western line being the richest. He also quoted Sir Roderick Murchison's words in 1864, in which that great *savant* denied the generally-believed assertion that he had predicted the finding of gold in Western Australia. Then followed a description of the various goldfields, including Dundas Hills, Yilgarn, Coolgardie, Murchison, Gascoyne, Pilbarra, Marble Bar, Bamboo Creek, and Kimberley. Mr. Calvert wound up his address with a comparison between Western Australia and South Africa. It appears that seventeen years elapsed before the latter fields had produced £200,000 worth of gold, while the former fields in the seventh year had exceeded that amount. Moreover, the output for the first seven years in Western Australia is more than double that of South Africa for the first seven years; and also in the first fourteen years Western Australia exceeds by £70,000 the output of South Africa; and this notwithstanding the fact that the former has been but slightly prospected and inefficiently worked.

In the discussion which followed, Mr. Matthew Macfie spoke hopefully of the water question, and would postpone railway construction until this problem had been effectually solved. He fully agreed with the speaker's statements regarding the auriferous wealth of the Colony, and strongly deprecated over-capitalisation of mines. Finally he advocated the sending of qualified experts, in order that genuine mines might be selected by English syndicates, and concluded by recalling a remark made to him by Sir Frederick Weld, to the effect that although it was said that Western Australia was nothing but sand, still he (Sir Frederick) had always contended that it was sand which would grow anything if *you only gave it water.*

In the course of the discussion Mr. Calvert alluded to worthless leases being made the basis of mining speculation, and the subject proved so attractive that an adjournment till Wednesday, the 31st inst., was agreed upon, when the topic will be resumed.

Whilst rejoicing in this manifestation of interest in Western Australian affairs, we fully appreciate the compliment paid to Mr. Calvert, and through him to the *West Australian Mining Register.*

IX—A MOMENTOUS QUESTION : WATER.

No problem in human economy is of greater antiquity than the Water Question. Moses was in grave perplexity at Mount Horeb, and only got over his difficulty with divine assistance. The Superintendent of Water Supply has Coolgardie on his mind, and it is interesting to note that the Lands Department appear to have taken a leaf out of the great Law Giver's book.

There are doubtless differences in the mode of procedure, and very possibly only a fractional proportion of faith on the part of the modern water-seekers ; but the same implement is used, viz., the Rod.

Our esteemed contemporary, the *Western Mail*, is rather sarcastic in its remarks upon the subject, and characterizes the system of finding water by means of a Divining Rod as a failure, except in its humorous aspect. It seems that the Rod and its Keeper have been perambulating the wilds of Coolgardie, and for a long time gave no indications of the whereabouts of water. At last however, they struck water ; but the fluid was salt, and the supply of this saline draught was at the limited rate of about a quart every five minutes. This is a little disheartening, and no doubt was a great disappointment to the keeper of this magic wand, more especially when disappointed Coolgardians declare that they could have got a supply of salt water without its assistance. We have no particulars upon which to form an opinion, and must content ourselves with an expression of sympathy. Still even in this country Divining Rods and their discoverers are apt to be taken with a grain of salt.

We have in old books of science, fantastic, alchemical notions of the middle ages; for the *savants* of that period firmly believed in the Divining Rod as an infallible test not only for water, but for minerals. A rod of this stamp would indeed be a boon on the Coolgardie field, especially if it possessed sufficient intelligence to discriminate between salt and fresh, and between gold and copper. This is not exacting a higher standard than that expected from any schoolboy who runs errands for his mother.

Dr. Brewer is very severe in his definition of a Divining Rod :—" A forked branch of hazel, suspended by two prongs between the balls of the thumbs. The inclination of the rod indicates the presence of water-springs, precious metal, *and anything else simpletons will pay for.*" Sir Walter Scott has immortalised Dousterswivel in " The Antiquary." The readers will doubtless remember that this gentleman was a German schemer who obtained money under the promise of finding hidden wealth by a Divining Rod.

A gentleman, who lived in Somersetshire a few years ago, relates that he lived on the side of a rocky hill in a house dependent on rain-water for its supply. One day his servants announced that a " Dowser " wished to see him. Not knowing what was meant by this term, he went to his door and met an old man who offered to find a spring by means of the "Dowsing-twig." On giving his assent, the man immediately went to a hawbush and cut a forked twig, which he trimmed to the proper size. He then began a slow march round the garden, followed by the gentleman and his family. To their surprise in reaching a certain spot they saw the twig twist round in his fingers and bend towards the ground. Here the "Dowser" declared water was certain to be found. And sure enough they came on a spring at a very shallow depth.

In writing to the *London Standard* the same authority states : " I have tried the experiment frequently in strange places, and without having the least idea where wells or springs might be, and invariably the twigs turned so vigorously towards the spot where water is, that it is with the utmost difficulty I could retain my hold on them." We do not profess much knowledge upon such an occult science as the above, but we are given to understand that it is based on a theory that certain plants, having a strong affinity for, or need of water, are promoted by some strange instinct to bend when in its proximity. Whatever grain of truth there may be in this assertion, it does not account for the finding of metals by the same means. In this case the keeper would be invaluable, for while the plant showed an affinity for water, the former would doubtless be possessed of a craving for gold, so strong as possibly to cause the twig to indicate another Bayley's Reward.

History is said to repeat itself, and here we have a curious instance. Timbuctoo, that strange and mysterious city of Central Africa, which was occupied on the 10th of January by Colonel Bonnier, in the name of the French Republic, and where a portion of his column met with serious disaster, was founded by the Touaregs in the 5th century. Not until the 14th century, however, did the fame of its wealth reach the ears of European merchants. It was then rich and prosperous, and known far and wide for its trade in gold and salt. And to-day the town of Timbuctoo does a notable business in gold, salt, and kola nut. It would therefore seem that gold and salt run in couples, and that salt is not altogether to be despised as an article of commerce.

Another very old-fashioned, but much more practical method of finding water, is by boring. The Artesian well is the modern type of those used in Artois, France, where they were first employed in Europe, but these wells were known in Egypt, China and elsewhere at a very ancient date. If at any place the strata bends into a trough or basin, with its concavity upwards, and if two impermeable beds are separated by one or more strata, which water can penetrate, then the rain will percolate into the porous beds at any point where an outcrop takes place, and, prevented from moving far up or down by the impermeable strata, will accumulate till it reaches the outcrops. If now a bore be made in the centre of the basin, the water will be forced up by that standing at a higher level than itself, and may reach, or even rise above the surface of the ground. This is roughly the principle of an artesian well, subject to certain variations. There has been a difference of opinion as to their feasibility in the Yilgarn Goldfield, of which Coolgardie forms an important section.

Speaking generally, however, one of the most notable physical features of Western Australia, and, indeed, all over the Island Continent, is the absence of rivers and surface waters. The scanty and intermittent rainfall does not account for this, because it is nowhere altogether wanting; and the water which does fall from the clouds should be amply sufficient to supply numerous lakes, and to fill many rivers and streams.

We find a reason for their extreme scarcity in the geological structure of the country, which presents for the most part a porous surface, quite unfavourable to the retention of water. Since evaporation accounts for but a fraction of the rainfall, we are driven to the conclusion that the water in seeking its level is received into great underground reservoirs, wherever impermeable rock favours its retention. Thus we may conclude that the geological and meteorological conditions of Western Australia are for the most part highly suitable for the sinking of artesian wells.

A considerable number have already been sunk, and attended with conspicuous success in the other Colonies. For example, as Dr. A. R. Wallace tells us, at the Buckalow Station, near the Stanley Range, close to the Boundary between New South Wales and South Australia, a copious flow was obtained at 160 ft. depth. In the cretacious deposits of Queensland, near Mount Wilson, a boring of 488 feet was made, and the water rose within 90 feet of the surface; while at Wee Watta, in a bore 144 feet deep, the water rose 26 feet above the surface, and discharged 60,000 gallons a day. But the most remarkable results have been obtained on the territory of our neighbour, South Australia, where, in some of the most arid districts, true artesian wells have been found. Thus in the ninety-mile desert, crossed by the Inter-Colonial Railway to Victoria, water was obtained in 1866, and flows above the surface. In the interior, along the Northern Telegraph Line, and Transcontinental Railway, there are already four large wells, the water from which flows above the surface in large quantities. At Hergott 100,000 gallons a day, at Coward, 1,250,000 gallons a day, at Strangways the same immense daily quantity, and at Mungamurtiemurtie 53,000 gallons a day, the last named being 580 miles from Port Augusta, or almost in the centre of the desert interior. The Water Conservation Department of the South Australian Government has now ten drills in constant use, capable of boring holes from three to thirteen inches in diameter, and to a depth of 3,000 feet.

We do not now refer to the works on the Irrigation Colonies of Mildura and Renmark on the Murray River, which are in full working order, and promise to yield abundant returns. All these scientific triumphs make us more and more sanguine regarding Western Australia. When a man is known to have great money-making powers, he is not likely to perish from hunger or thirst. And so it is with a country. When it is proved to be rich in precious metal, capital will send forth brains, muscle, and machinery to transform the desert. It is no new project either. Seven hundred years before the Christian era Isaiah wrote these words: "I will open rivers in high places, and fountains in the midst of the valleys; I will make the wilderness a pool of water, and the dry land springs of water. I will plant in the wilderness the cedar, and the myrtle, and the oil tree; I will set in the desert the fir tree and the pine." Isaiah was a prophet, and we look for a fulfilment of his words in some of the arid wastes of Western Australia.

X.—CONCERNING OUR CHANGE OF NAME.

" O be some other name," cries Juliet to Romeo, in Shakespeare's incomparable play. Then she goes on to exclaim :—" What's in a name ? That which we call a rose ; by any other name would smell as sweet ; " and so on. After a few prosperous months of literary life, we have determined to change the name of *Calvert's West Australian Mining Register."* Not that we are by any means ashamed of its former; and not that we contemplate, for a moment, altering the line of policy which we have up to now adopted. But we have felt that perhaps the designation we had chosen was a shade too narrow to indicate our scope.

We shall henceforth appear as the *" West Australian Review,"* and we do not hesitate to call attention to the artistic headpiece which crowns our journal. It is the work of *Cynicus,* and is designed to illustrate some of the riches with which Western Australia has been prodigally endowed.

Perhaps there is something in a name after all. In olden days some names were supposed to strike fear into the hearts of those who heard them spoken. A few may be mentioned. Attila was a bogie man to the latter Romans. Bob, son of Odin, was used (Sir William Temple tells us) by the Gothic captains in order to scare their soldiers. Warton tells us that the Dutch frightened their children with the same word ; and we have all heard of

"Bo to a goose." The name of Bonaparte was, early in the century, a name of terror throughout Europe; and Camden, in his " Remains," reminds us that the proud appellation of " Cœur de Lion " was employed by the Saracens as a name of dread and terror. Says Gibbon, in his " Decline and Fall of the Roman Empire," regarding the lion-hearted monarch of England :—"His tremendous name was employed by the Syrian mothers to silence the infants ; and if a horse suddenly started from the way his rider was wont to exclaim, ' Dost thou think King Richard is in the bush." Tamerlane's name kept the Persians *in terrorem ;* and going back once more to the greatest poet who ever lived in any age or in any country, Shakespeare, "the myriad - minded and the honey-tongued " makes the outraged Lucrece exclaim :—" The nurse to still her child will tell my story ; and fright her crying babe with Tarquin's name."

"Give a dog a bad name and hang him " is a well-known adage. To a great extent this proverb has been verified in regard to the early history of Western Australia, when for a period she had reason to dread the presence of the goal-bird and the gibbet. She has fought through the troubles of those days by the aid of the brave men domiciled on her stubborn acres, and now England rings with the tidings of her unsuspected wealth ; unsuspected—that is—by even her own inhabitants, but foreseen by the light of science in the person of the veteran mining geologist, John Calvert.

Australia herself had several cognomens before she was so called. Terra Australis, Terra Incognita, Terra

Aurifera, Jave la grande, were a few of her ancient titles, till Tasman christened her New Holland. We almost forget who baptised her "Australia." It may have been at the suggestion of Flinders.

May we be pardoned if we introduce a curious incident in the life of Lord Palmerston, illustrating the wonderful readiness of that great statesman. Palmer, the poisoner, had made the name of the town of Rugeley notorious. The citizens sent a deputation to the Prime Minister, requesting that the name of the place should be changed. His lordship naturally recognised a dangerous precedent, and demurred. "What would you say to calling it '*Palmer's Town*,' he remarked; and they realised that on similar principles Palmerston might find it desirable to change *his own name*.

We may have rambled a little in the course of this intimation and apology, but can only hope that the "*West Australian Review*" may never have cause to regret its re-christening. Under a new guise may we hope to give increased satisfaction to the public who have taken an interest in our pages. We know full well that we are not "everybody's paper." We deal with a specialty, and in one sense we are quite exceptional. We have ventured to start a newspaper in London, devoted entirely to one distant and little known colony. Nevertheless we have great reasons for thankfulness, both to the press and the public, that we have been enabled to surmount our initial difficulties, and we trust go forward in a sanguine hope of doing our duty and achieving eventual success.

XI.—A NOBLE SPECIMEN OF WESTRALIA'S WEALTH.

For the last ten days a metallic display of great significance has been on view at Messrs. Spink & Sons' establishment, in Gracechurch Street. It consists of forty-one bars of gold, weighing 6,886 ounces, and forty-four specimens of quartz, giving 760 ounces—the whole being valued at £35,000. It attracted the gaze of thousands, including bankers, bullionists, mineralogists and others; and set many people wondering at the marvellous wealth of Coolgardie. We cannot but reiterate our profound satisfaction that the Western Australian Government has acted in a wise spirit of enterprise and liberality, and we feel assured that their colony will reap a well-deserved harvest of advantage.

Few people realize how largely our prosperity is affected by the vicissitudes of gold mining, and it may be interesting to roughly sketch how the world has been supplied during the last forty-three years.

After the Australian discoveries, and between the years 1851 and 1860, the average annual production throughout civilized countries was valued at about $28\tfrac{1}{2}$ millions sterling, according to the acknowledged authority, Dr. Soetbeer. In the next decade, the average fell to $26\tfrac{1}{2}$ millions sterling; and between 1881 and 1894 it further fell to $19\tfrac{1}{2}$ millions—a decline of more than one-third from the highest point of production. Since 1885 three quite new sources of supply have been discovered. South Africa, which is now yielding about 5½ millions; Western Australia, which last year produced about half-a-million; and India, which has yielded about the same amount. The development of the first-mentioned colony has been quite phenomenal. Seven years ago the entire output of South Africa was about 20,000 ounces, roughly valued at £70,000. And yet she has actually, since 1886, added £18,000,000 to the world's stock of gold.

At present the production of gold is rapidly rising—partly owing to these three discoveries, but by no means altogether attributable to these discoveries alone. We have more than once insisted on the enormous waste of precious metal in all parts of the world, caused by unskilful treatment and inadequate machinery; and we feel assured that it is the gradual adoption in South Africa of the most improved methods that has enabled her to show such a magnificent output. Not that she crowns the list; by no means. Australia is still to the front, as the undernoted statistics will show. In 1893 we find that there were four great sources from which the bulk of the world's gold was won, namely:—Australia, South Africa, Russia and the United States. There were other minor sources, of which India is one. The yield of these four was as follows, according to the best authorities:—

Australia	£6,560,000
South Africa	5,623,250
Russia	5,394,170
United States	5,050,000

The total product of the world in 1893, including about three-and-a-half millions from various other quarters, amounted to £26,228,600; and this showed an increase of about two-and-a-half millions over the product of 1892.

It can hardly be doubted that gold will always dominate the course of exchange and the price of commodities, as long as England remains mono-metallic; nay, even if she became bi-metallic, the yellow metal would probably hold the mastery over the commercial world. Not only is gold the great medium of exchange, but it is a vastly important article of commerce, and the chief reason of its great value as a monetary medium is its immense utility for many other purposes.

We find that gold, silver, copper, tin, lead, and even iron have been used as a means of exchange in all historical ages. With the exception of the latter these metals are all peculiarly indestructible, and undergo but little deterioration when handled or hoarded up. In fact some metals seem to have been by nature singularly adapted for employment as money, either from their malleability, colour, density, hardness, or other causes.

We may at once dismiss iron as a money-metal, though, from the statements of Aristotle, Pollux and others, it was extensively employed for coinage in early times. Not a single specimen of such money is now known to exist, because, of course, the metal has naturally rusted away. Up till quite lately, however, iron was used in Japan for small coinage, and small bars are still used in trading by the natives of Central Africa.

Lead has often been used in currency, and is occasionally so mentioned by Greek and Latin writers. Moreover, so late as 1635, leaden bullets were used for change at the rate of a farthing a-piece in the State of Massachusetts. It is still current in Burmah, being passed by weight for small payments, but it is obviously too soft for coining in its pure state.

Tin has been employed as money at various times, and in 1680 tin farthings were struck by Charles II., a stud of copper being inserted in the middle of each, so as to hinder counterfeiting. In the reign of William and Mary (1691) halfpence and farthings were likewise struck out of this metal.

Copper is in many respects well adapted for coining. The earliest Hebrew coins were of copper, and until B.C. 269, *Aes*—an impure copper—was the currency of Rome.

Silver has been coined in all ages, and may be said to take the middle place between copper and gold. When suitably alloyed it is sufficiently hard to stand severe wear and tear, and it well deserves the second place in the monetary system.

Platinum was attempted by the Russian Government in 1828, but many objections presented themselves, into which we need not enter; and nickel is still used in alloy by the United States Government for 2 and 5 cent pieces.

Gold—the monarch of metals—possesses qualities quite unparalleled among those we have enumerated. Its rich and brilliant colour, its high specific gravity, its unmistakeable ring, its wonderful malleability, its freedom from corrosion, make gold stand at a far higher level than any other of the precious metals. "*L'or est une chimère*"—"Gold is a chimera"—are words occurring in the celebrated opera of "Robert le Diable." We cannot consent to this. Gold is not a vain and foolish fancy, but a great reality.

The world well knows this, and hence Western Australia is a centre of interest at the present time. With every disadvantage to contend against—want of men, want of money, want of water, and a thousand other obstacles to fight with—she has achieved wonders in the way of gold-mining; and we do not hesitate to say that if the same energy, capital, skill and advertisement, which have made South Africa prolific, were applied to "Westralia," she would prove a worthy rival to her Colonial sister.

We can only hope, now that the riches of Coolgardie gold-field are known in England, more attention will be directed to opening up the other vast auriferous resources of the colony. Can it be for a moment supposed that this mine—accidentally come upon by Messrs. Bayley and Ford—is an *isolated* reef, or that it is the richest reef in Western Australia? Such a theory would be preposterous. To imagine that any two men could go out into a wilderness, measuring millions of acres, and within a few weeks discover the *only rich* reef, or the *richest* reef, in that vast district, would be to say that it is quite a simple matter to find the proverbial needle in a haystack.

No. Western Australia has displayed a fair sample of her treasures, and she invites the world to come out and help her to find them. Distant she is no doubt, but science has reduced distance to a minimum ; and scientific skill, backed up by capital, will yet disclose the buried millions of bullion which lie sleeping in the reefs, which stretch over a thousand miles from Kimberley, in the North, to Dundas Hills, on the South. Western Australia is a land pregnant with gold, and a few more years will show how high she ranks among the territories which supply the raw material of the world's wealth.

XII.—BARS AND QUARTZ FOR THE IMPERIAL INSTITUTE.

Last week we alluded to the display of gold in bars and quartz at the establishment of Messrs. Spink, in Gracechurch Street. There it was viewed by thousands whose daily duty takes them into the heart of the City of London. No more appropriate place could have been chosen for the purpose of exhibiting this splendid trophy of West Australian gold. But there are many who "never go east of Temple Bar," except on such rare occasions as Dividend Day at the Bank of England, and such like. It was therefore but natural that Messrs. Spink should give the dwellers in the West End an opportunity of seeing the bullion in their well known Piccadilly house.

Messrs. Spink inform us that many hundreds of ladies and gentlemen, representing such of the rank and fashion of the metropolis as are at present in town, responded to their invitation to a private view of the bars and quartz in question. The exhibition was held in the rear of the establishment, where the firm happen to have a room well fitted for the purpose. It is lighted from the roof by ample skylights, and was plentifully adorned with flowers. At the end, on cushions of silk plush, lay thirty-five thousand pounds worth of bullion. One man only seemed to take but little interest in the display. He seemed more taken up with the appearance of the visitors. As yet he does not appear to have recognized any familiar faces, and it is to be hoped that his active assistance will not be needed. Two others of his profession were on guard outside in uniform.

There was also on view a fine assortment of jewels, brilliants, emeralds, and pearls, roughly estimated to be worth about £15,000. These were examined with interest, and the tenth commandment sadly shattered we fear. A good many of those who attended the show of gold, diamonds and so forth, were glad to turn from the contemplation of filthy lucre to the magnificent and unique collection of English medals and jettons, commemorating famous battles by land and sea, celebrated statesmen, naval and military commanders, poets, painters, and savants. This splendid collection was illustrative of English history back to the 15th century, and among other rarities in gold we noticed the following medals: Lord Essex, Sir Thomas Fairfax, the famous "Blake" medal, Cromwell, "Culloden" medal, Louisbourg, etc. The lot were valued at £12,500.

Till Friday, the 27th, the gold will remain on view, and next day, in charge of three assistants, and the inevitable detective, it will be conveyed in a covered van, and handed over to the representative of the West Australian Government at the Imperial Institute.

XIII.—GOLD TO THE RESCUE: A COMPARISON.

In the course of his speech at the opening dinner of "Anglo-African's Writers' Club," Mr. H. Rider Haggard, the hon. president, in speaking of the disasters and troubles which preceded South Africa's rise to her present position of splendid prosperity, rose to considerable eloquence. The Boers had just utterly defeated our troops. "Never, gentlemen," he said, "if I live to the age of 100, shall I forget that scene upon the market square in Newcastle, when the news of our surrender went home to the intelligence of the three or four thousand refugees loyal Boers, English, and natives who were gathered there that night. Never do I wish to see such another scene, or to hear such curses as were uttered by these ruined, dishonoured men. I confess that I felt it myself. I felt it so much that I left South Africa, which at the time I did not consider a fit home for an Englishman. Then followed dark days, etc." And then Mr. Haggard goes on to say:"Then light arose in darkness, and that light, the Johannesburg gold. The naked veld, which I have trekked over in an ox-waggon, was proved to cover wealth in countless millions, and where, but some few years since, there was nothing to be seen but troops of wandering game, a great city has arisen, peopled by Englishmen and financed with English capital. Thus was the balance restored, and the evil of the past, if not undone, at least put on the way of undoing." So much for the celebrated novelist's interesting retrospect of South Africa, its sorrows, and its ultimate triumph, through the discovery of all powerful gold.

Let us turn to the financial statement of Sir John Forrest, K.C.M.G., made January, 1892, in which the Premier of Western Australia uses words of very similar import. "I know," he says, "that in a large portion of the colony there is a dark cloud hanging over and darkening the very doors and houses of the people. The drought is not over yet. Certainly there are signs of its dispersal, but, the end is not yet, and whatever the results may be, years and years must pass before persons who have invested their capital and embarked their fortunes in that part of the colony, can recover what they have lost. But, while we know this, and the fact appeals to us in more ways than one, yet the colony, notwithstanding this calamity, has prospered and is progressing. I can only put down the improvement in our position to the gold discoveries, which have come to the rescue. The impetus which has been given, by the discovery of gold and the development of our mineral resources, has done away with the great depression which otherwise must have followed the drought in the north.

We deem it a matter of no small significance to note points of similarity in these remarks by two men eminently well-fitted to speak on their respective topics. Sir John Forrest's speech was made just two and a quarter years before that of Mr. Haggard. The Premier may be said to have spoken prophetically, the Novelist retrospectively. "Gold to the rescue" is the burden of both orations. We cannot but wonder if Sir John foresaw, or anticipated, the extraordinary wealth of gold now revealed by Coolgardie; or if in his mind's eye he saw Western Australia represented in the Imperial Institute by £35,000 worth of bullion, and all the great London newspapers recounting the richness of her goldfields. We venture to think the Premier's hopes of two years ago have been more than realised. No man, however, knew better the possibilities of these inland deserts. Twenty five years ago the Hon. John Forrest, pioneer and explorer, with his brother Alexander as second in command, traversed these wilds and encountered the perils Eyre had experienced thirty years previously. He, who led three expeditions into the interior, may well now have the chief voice in the administration of Western Australia.

We do not for a moment suppose, however, that Sir John Forrest, even during his last and most arduous journey into the interior, ever suspected the presence of gold in these regions. The results of this expedition are thus summed up in his own words: "The whole of the country from Champion Bay to the head of the Murchison is admirably suited for pastoral settlement, and in a very short time will be taken up and stocked; indeed some has already been occupied * * * * * The general character of this immense tract is a gently undulating spinifex desert. It is lightly wooded, and there is a great absence of any large timber."

Whether or not, the then Hon. John Forrest, of the Survey Department, ever dreamt of the riches of the Murchison fields in those distant days is no business of ours. Suffice it to say that as an explorer he has gained imperishable laurels.

XIV—SHALL WESTRALIA FEDERATE?

We cannot help being interested in the address given by Sir Henry Parkes, at the Perth Town Hall. It is reported in *oratio obliqua*; hence we lose much of its force. It is not for us to dictate; nevertheless we cannot but express our opinion that it would be well for our esteemed contemporary, the *Western Mail*, if such an important speech as that of Sir Henry Parkes was reported in the first person, and exactly as spoken.

It is not easy for us, living at the other side of the world, and knowing but little of Australian ways and manners, to give an opinion as to the momentous question of " The Federation of the Australian Colonies." Nevertheless, on the principle that the onlooker sometimes sees most of the game, we will venture to make a remark or two on the somewhat fluent speech of Sir Henry Parkes. We pass over the preamble, which recapitulates several items of Australian history, and some very interesting statistics. And we do likewise with some extremely flattering allusions to William Charles Wentworth, Mr. O'Shannassy, Sir Charles Gavan Duffy and others. Sir Henry, however, becomes gradually a shade facetious, if not flippant, and at last settles down to business.

He gives us some examples First the German Confederation. No doubt Prince Bismarck's genius exhibited itself wonderfully here. But we venture to say that the conditions differed very much from those which exist now in our Australian Colonies. The German Empire, surrounded by armed hosts and in a constant attitude of defence, cannot be safely contrasted with a huge, thinly populated dependency of England, despised and disdained by the greediest adventurers that ever swept the sea: the Spanish, the Portuguese and the Dutch. To bring into union the German Empire was an absolute necessity. The German generals recognised this, and accomplished the design. Still, we fail to appreciate the force of his argument, nor do we appreciate the analogy between Australia and Germany. We need not trouble our readers with statistics. They are at every one's command. Nevertheless we may remind Sir Henry Parkes that Prussia alone, with an area of 137,000 miles, has 29 millions of inhabitants; Bavaria 6 millions; Wurtemburg 2 millions; Saxony, 3 millions; Baden, 1,600,000. We need not enumerate the other German States. Their population reaches 50 millions. To compare the countries is evidently ridiculous. Then again, Sir Henry talks of the United States of America. God forbid that Australia should follow their miserable example. The brand of Cain is on the great Republic, as I think Mr. Wakefield said in the "Nineteenth Century" a year or two ago. And why? Perhaps because they have no morality, no power of government, no respect for law; nothing but a miserable adulation for the dollar. We question if there is a civilised country in the world that stands so low among the nations as America? Corrupt to the core; inheriting the curse of slave owning; still keeping alive the miserable party-riot, dignified by the name of the American War. Why to see the so-called veterans, belonging to that curious organisation called the 'Grand Army of the Republic,' is a painful example of human weakness and little self-conceit. The Americans have deceived themselves, and the truth is not in them.

Sir Henry then refers to the Dominion of Canada, and, so far as can be gleaned from the slender report of his speech, makes a few fairly sensible remarks. He does not, however, clear up the stupendous difficulty which arises in America, through the seat of Government at Washington being so remote from the Western States. It is pretty severe on a United States Senator to have to make a two or three thousand miles journey in order to represent his constituents. But we do not hope to take an example from America. Surely, Sir Henry cannot suggest that we should copy the very worst form of Republic Government which the world has ever seen. Let us hope not. It may be that the shores of Western Australia are without lighthouses and beacons. That is perhaps a sad state of affairs, but we scarcely think that Federation will illuminate her coasts. Nay, every night that the Western Australian goes to sleep can we not safely send up an earnest prayer of thankfulness that he was born under the "Union Jack." Gracious heavens, think of lighting up the coast of Western Australia. No. Western Australia has kept herself clear of the recent woes which have beset some adjacent colonies. Western Australia has happily bided her time; and now, because she has shown her metal, is she to be honoured by admission to the society of, and invited to take part with, the other Colonies. "Brethren in blood," says Sir Henry, but surely that can be said likewise of the Americans.

Doubtless, now that Western Australia has not only remained solvent, but shows great promise of abundant wealth, the other Colonies are naturally a little anxious for her company. We have seen something like this in England. "Birth, genius, or a million will admit to London Society," said the late Lord Beaconsfield. Western Australia has been a modest wench, and can wait.

XV.—UNITED WE STAND.

A contemporary says :—" Vice-Admiral Sir John Hopkins, commanding the British cruisers *Blake* and *Tartar*, which have been visiting Roslin, yesterday evening, made a statement, says Reuter, to a number of Press reporters, that the distance which parts England and America lessens every day. The ties which unite them grow every day stronger. Against this silent and inevitable drift of things the spirit of narrow isolation, on either side of the Atlantic, struggles in vain. It is possible that the two branches of the English people may remain for ever separate political existences. It is likely though that the older of them may again break in twain, and that the English in the Pacific may assert as distinct a national life as the two English peoples on either side of the Atlantic. I trust that in the near future a real and higher Federation of our naval forces may occur, and that the glorious flags of your country and mine may guarantee abiding peace and protection throughout the world."

Now, regarding the statement of this British Admiral, we have a few words to say. None more than ourselves would rejoice to see a coalition of English-speaking races. Such an alliance—if it could be brought about—would undoubtably be the Head Arbiter among the nations. But is such a thing possible ? We think not. What is the American Republic composed of ? Are we wrong in saying that the United States is at present a horrible hotbed of vice, iniquity and evil government. May we not likewise say, that, although called the " United States," they have no " unity " whatever. Their great men—there are a few of them—for example J. Russell Lowell, Longfellow, Washington Irving, Oliver Wendell Holmes, and perhaps another dozen or so, have always bewailed the horrors which exist under the present style of American Government. We know what wickedness is in London. Multiply that a thousand fold, and we have some faint conception of the quagmire of vice in which the United States Republic is content to wallow, all rolling themselves in filth and corruption for the sake of the Almighty Dollar. Of course their women are innocent and exempt, and occasionally fling themselves into the arms of our impecunious aristocracy.

Take not example Australians from that great American Republic, rushing to its ruin. Cling to England in the meantime. She has much money to lend ; she has many sons and daughters to send to you. It is hard in a measure to lead our rambling discourse back ; but we look upon Western Australia as the coming colony of the world. Far greater is her prospect than that of Cape Colony. Glance at the two territories on the map and judge. Compare their magnitude. There are of course very few men with the exceptional advantages of Mr. Cecil Rhodes. Money rarely runs with brains. But with such as Sir John Forrest, and others who assist him, we doubt not that the ultimate success and triumph of Western Australia is secured.

Sir John Hopkins's remarks are a little vague, as reported. He talks about the distance between America and England "lessening every day." Of course he alludes to our better knowledge of how to build such steamships as are independent of Atlantic storms. The War of Independence, to our view, proved that for the moment England had a weak-headed king and a rascally government. Burke, our undoubtedly greatest orator of the period, thundered against our folly. 'Twas hopeless. Mark Antony cried to the Roman *populus*, according to Shakespeare, "Ye Blocks, ye Stones, ye worse than senseless things." Burke did his best, yet we lost America. After all, we on this side can do little more than advise. Perhaps it is our province also to entertain, in some small degree, those readers who scan our pages, and help to make it worth while to publish our paper.

So far we have been discursive; but when we contemplate the splendid prospects of Western Australian lands, we naturally look round on our own country going to absolute destruction in many quarters. We quote from a Parliamentary Blue Book, and beg our Western Australian readers to judge how we are fixed. Diplomatists and Economists "read, mark, learn and inwardly digest" the following. It is the report of Mr. Hunter Pringle in respect to an agricultural district almost within walking distance of the Bank of England.

"The ensuing year (1894) will witness a downfall more disastrous in its consequences than any stranger to Essex could possibly apprehend. If three-fourths of the farmers, who have served notices to quit in 1894, act upon them, thousands of acres will be left tenantless ; and it requires a stretch of imagination more than I can make to suppose that new tenants will be found."

Bankruptcy, loss, ruin, weeds, and waste are at present the state of affairs in some parts of England. We suggest, with all deference, that Western Australia may do much to help us. She has *too* much land ; we have too many people. England has gold in her vaults, safes, and strong places, amply fitted to release some of the gold from the Western Australian deserts. Able to fit out such expeditions as would, not only find their way into every corner of the colony, but would also open up her water-springs, and preserve her rainfall.

Australia has suffered in one peculiar respect. She has never needed England's interference for warlike purposes. She would have been discovered long before if she had lain the line for Alexander's or Cæsar's march, and we would know more of her interior. Brave men have risked and lost their lives in the attempt to penetrate and explore her deserts. Money is lavishly expended on war. But the poor Australian savage, with his wonderful, and most strangely devised weapon —the Boomerang—has never been considered worthy of the Maxim, the Gatling or the Nordenfeldt. Dirk Hartog did something, Dampier did more, Tasman did all that Dutch courage could do ; but after all Cook gave England Australia, which she will yet find her very grandest possession. Grand, because loyal and law-abiding : rich in herself by the heritage of nature.

XVI.—THE INSTITUTE OF MINING ENGINEERS SEEK INFORMATION.

All contributions to our knowledge on the all-engrossing subject of Western Australia are likely to be welcome. It is only natural. Most other countries are in the meantime "played out." Western Australia has patiently waited her turn: and it has come. She now has her innings, and it looks as if she was going to make top score. It is quite possible that the magnificent exhibition of gold, in the shape of bars and ores, in the windows of a leading firm in Gracechurch Street (Messrs. Spinks) might have led the public to say: "Western Australia has been pushed into a corner; she is short of money, and is now on the Boom." We cannot blame anyone for entertaining such a thought: the advertisement was palpable, tremendous, magnificent. But let us explain the why and the wherefore of the whole affair.

Western Australia was wretchedly represented in the Imperial Institute; and we, for our part, thought it was a mighty pity that such should be the case. We said so. The gold came, and was exhibited. The Colonial Government behaved handsomely, if they acted tardily, and so it came about that the name of Coolgardie became almost an equivalent for Western Australia.

A very high tribute to the absorbing interest which has been awakened in Western Australia was accorded on Friday, however, at a large and representative gathering of Mining Engineers in St. George's Street, Westminster. The ostensible object of the meeting was to hear a paper read by Mr. R. Herbert Lapage, who had just returned from Coolgardie. He did not read his own paper, which is much to be regretted. Although Mr. Walton Browne, the Secretary, endeavoured to do it justice, "the paper," as Sir Malcolm Fraser very truly put it, "lost half its force." Indeed, had not most of the members been supplied with printed copies it would have run the risk of losing *all* its force. As may well be supposed, the only portion of the paper of any value or interest was that which dealt with the author's personal knowledge and experience. The rest could have been easily dispensed with, since the matter is at our disposal in handbooks and year-books. Nevertheless this congregation of Mining Engineers was an occasion of great value and momentous importance to the colony of Western Australia. In our opinion no other meeting has so strongly illustrated the growing enthusiasm which England is beginning to evince regarding the splendid prospects of her youngest independent colony.

The Chairman of the meeting was Mr. Cochrane, one of the best known men in English mining circles, and it need scarcely be said that he filled the post with conspicuous tact and ability. Mr. Lapage, as we have stated, did not read his paper. It was a pity we think; for although he modestly disclaimed any pretention to rhetorical powers, still in his subsequent answers he displayed a self-command and fluency for which he would have scarcely given himself credit.

Sir Malcolm Fraser delivered a terse and telling address, giving a resumé of his wide and long colonial experience, and tracing the marvellous growth of the colony. Professor Boyd Dawkins spoke upon the coal question; and Professor Hull upon the discovery of the Kimberley Field by the late Mr. Hardman. He described him as the first discoverer of gold in Western Australia in 1885. It happened, however, that there was present John Calvert, the veteran mining geologist, who was able to state that he found gold on the Murchinson in 1847. "A magnificently preserved specimen of the old pioneer," said the chairman, when the acclamations which greeted the conclusion of John Calvert's exposition on meteoric waters had ceased. Then Mr. Moreing, speaking on the dearth of water in Coolgardie district, actually made the statement that the Government took pains to frustrate the finding of water. According to his gospel, if a man sunk a well and found water, the authorities would claim it and prevent its being used. This assertion, remaining uncontradicted for a time, aroused the very natural indignation of one gentleman present, who impeached the Government of the Colony in strong terms. When the contradiction came Mr. Moreing had vanished, which was to be regretted.

Mr. Albert F. Calvert's remarks on the paper were received with applause, and have been fully reported by our esteemed contemporaries, *The Mining Journal* and *The Mining World*.

Among the other speakers were Sir Charles Crawford, Messrs. A. G. Charlton, E. Bainbridge, Jeremiah Head, J. G. Binns, Hughes, Stoneham, Martin, Dr. Woodward, and others. One speaker made the remark that, so far as he could see, history was, as usual, repeating herself, and Western Australia was destined to match South Africa as a land of gold and precious stones. Let us hope his prediction will be verified.

XVII.—A UNITED AUSTRALIA?

Sydney, June 14.

"Sir George Dibbs has forwarded to the Hon. J. B. Paterson, Premier of Victoria, an important letter concerning Federation. His consideration of Federation, especially during the recent banking crisis, has led him to the conclusion that it would be easier first to completely unify the interests of Victoria and New South Wales, and then to attract the other colonies into such union. "It is not," he says, "a question of annexation, but of partnership." The proposal of the convention would necessitate 744 State legislators and 189 joint legislators, 933 in all, with eight Governors and fifty-six Ministers, while the Colonies would retain their debts, railways, &c. Sir George Dibbs then proceeds to urge that it would be more beneficial to pool the debts, railways, and national establishments generally of the colonies. He suggests that New South Wales and Victoria could arrange the terms of a union of interests more speedily than if the other Colonies were to enter at the outset.

Thus runs *Reuter's* despatch. We quite agree with Sir George Dibbs. By all means let New South Wales and Victoria make the experiment. Western Australia will, we fancy, take leave to look on and see how Federation works. Sadly handicapped as she has been, since the days when Captain Sterling initiated the Swan River Settlement, she has hitherto managed to hold her own.

Phenomenal success, either among men or nations, provokes question and arouses suspicion. But it soon passes off, when reiterated assertions are found to be true.

Still, looking at Federation from a general point of view, we quite fail to see why Western Australia should in the meantime be included in the scheme. The writer has at the present time the privilege to know a lady who lived in comparative affluence in the city of Bath. She is now practically a pauper. And why, because she unfortunately held shares in a Victorian Bank. "Pay £60 10s. a quarter, or forfeit your shares" came in the shape of a summons from Melbourne. She had no alternative. And this then is the chief colony which proposes to bolster itself up through an alliance with Western Australia. Companions in distress are New South Wales and Victoria!

Modesty certainly has been the distinguishing character of Western Australia, and she has earned her reward. Such men as Sir John Forrest are not readily influenced. They are made of that stern stuff which founds, upholds, and builds up nations. Born in the colony, brought up in the colony, and himself having surveyed her dreary deserts, such a man is eminently fitted to hold the reins of Government. Long may he continue to hold them; and it is not for a moment to be apprehended that he has not carefully weighed in his mind the subject of Federation. It is not for us to dictate. We see things from a long distant point of view. But, notwithstanding the many leagues which

F

separate us, our heart beats in unison with our brothers of the Antipodes. Western Australia is in our opinion safe as to her future, in spite of sneers regarding recent loans. We have never hesitated to pronounce her always safe and solvent, confident as we are in the marvellous wealth of her lands, however sterile. Let her motto be not, "Advance Australia," but "Reviresco." And we hope she will in the meantime keep herself free from her neighbours, who are all too anxious, we imagine, to share her riches.

To revert for a moment to the subject of an Australian Commonwealth, we would remind our readers that about three years have elapsed since the Sydney Convention, when certain proposals were put forward.

The *Pall Mall Gazette* says that "A year is in the history of a country as an hour is in the life of a man." This is something like the truth, and Sir George Dibbs is more or less to be congratulated for having seized the opportunity. He recognizes—and he is not wide of the mark—that Victoria and New South Wales are the key to the situation. Two-thirds of the population, and two-thirds of Australian wealth, undoubtedly count for much. The unification of these two colonies, under one Viceroy and one Parliament, would almost mean forcing the sister colonies to follow suit. We do not for an instant wish to deny Sir George all the credit due to him in regard to statesmanship and diplomacy. The customs tariff, one joint debt, one defence administration, one viceroy and one parliament reads well, sounds well, and would, we suppose, be a good thing on the whole, if it could be well managed. But, as a contemporary points out, New South Wales is a Free Trade Colony, while Victoria is intensely protective. Here comes in a serious difficulty. Mr. Hofmeyr has proposed a scheme, which, if adopted, we should set up Free Trade within the Empire with an *ad valorem* duty of $2\frac{1}{2}$ per cent. against the world. This gentleman, we are told, is now on his way to the Ottawa Conference, where it is to be hoped he will find those, not only open to conviction, but willing to be convinced.

Meantime, as a contemporary points out, the colonies are ridiculously over-legislated. The Sydney Convention proposed 933 legislators from a population of 3,000,000.

However, we take leave to stick to our opinion, and sincerely hope that Western Australia will adhere to her present policy, and retain at the helm of Government those men to which she owes her present position of honour and prosperity.*

---

* Since the article was written the Editor thinks that this is an exaggeration.

XVIII.—LAW-ABIDING AUSTRALIA: LAWLESS AMERICA.

We have occasionally in these columns compared the Peace of Australia with the War of America. We have been accused of speaking somewhat harshly of the condition of the so-called Great Republic. But we ask our readers to mark how our predictions have been justified. The United States of America are on the brink of Civil War, and, in our opinion, this next war will shatter the Union.

Stars and stripes are all very well in their way. Good things to pray for, sing about, and occasionally fight for. Still if " the Great Republic " cannot enforce her laws, and if Washington is confessedly incapable of governing Chicago, the American flag will soon be the laughing stock of the nations. Doubtless it would be well if the people who use the English language were joined in one great federation, bound by treaty to arbitrate, so as to preserve law, order, and, above all things, Peace. But look at America at the present moment. From the Atlantic to the Pacific we hear of nothing but rebellion. Why, we ask ourselves, is this great nation incapable of self-control ? The heritage of the slavery curse must be first taken into account. This led the Americans of old to have a contempt for human life and personal liberty. Then came that most horrible of Wars, lasting from April the 15th, 1861, till April 14th, 1865, four years all but a day; and their dead are buried in no less than seventy-nine national cemeteries. Most of these are in the Southern States. We mention two only of these awful graveyards. In Arlington, Virginia, 16,264 bodies lie;—4,349 are unknown. In Beaufort, South Carolina, 9,241 dead men were buried, 4,493 unknown. In all 300,000 men repose in guarded graveyards of the Great Republic, many of whom perished in the loathsome prisons constructed or contrived during the most abominable war of history. For example, Andersonville, in the State of Georgia, has a cemetery which contains 13,714 graves; and Salisbury 12,126, the majority unknown. It is impossible to survey these events, and glance at the tidings flashed across the Atlantic Ocean, without a feeling of congratulation regarding our own well-ruled and self-governed Colonies. No envy, hatred in malice, disturbs the peace of Western Australia. She has given our Foreign Office little or no trouble, and she has put England to no serious expense. Hampered, as she is, by her enormous bulk of territory, and troubled as she is by lack of water, we hear of nothing but the natural cry for men and women to inhabit her lands. The mineral resources of Western Australia have been abundantly tested and abundantly proved. Half a century ago John Calvert landed on her shores, and found gold where he knew it would occur. That it is there is an indisputed fact. And what next ? British Capital must flow towards the youngest and biggest dependency of England. British brain and muscle must follow in its train, and the vast area of 1,600,000 square miles must be developed.

Such things, however, cannot be done in a moment. The very name of Australia brings to mind ruined homes and hungering children. But for the faults of the Eastern Colonies Western Australia cannot be held responsible. With such men as Robinson and Forrest she can afford to feel comfortable. The former in touch with England, and the latter calmly watching and guiding the progress of his native colony. Jealousy and suspicion Western Australia is bound to encounter. It is the fate of every successful nation, and every successful man; but there cannot be a shadow of doubt but that Cinderella is destined to wear the glass slipper.

It is extremely painful for us in England to note the discontent which seems to exist in the North and North West Districts of West Australia. The Nor' West suffers under tremendous disadvantages, and Perth seems to be to a certain extent oblivious to the needs of Roebourne and the neighbourhood. Now it is not our place to interfere with West Australian politics; still we cannot close our eyes to the fact that there is a pressing need for development in that direction. "Coolgardie, Murchison and Dundas Hill are the only gold-finders worthy of a trial," says the *Nor' West Times* of May 12th.

Now we do not intend to draw a comparison between the Northern and the Southern districts of Western Australia. This we will say, however. Parallel reefs of gold run straight through the country from North to South.

Mr. John Calvert, a man who for half-a-century has devoted his attention to the question of finding gold, has not only demonstrated on paper, but proved by production of rich ore, that gold reefs run from north to south through the colony of West Australia. Suspecting as he did in New South Wales that the reef tended westward, he investigated for himself, and proved his theory through explorations on both the Ashburton and the Murchison River.

He is now an octogenarian, and little more can be expected of him. Still he was able to speak a few words the other day at the meeting of the Federated Institute of Mining Engineers at Westminster.

The North and Nor' West tell us that they have reasons to feel aggrieved. We can only say that the Government of the Colony of Western Australia are doing the very best in their power, but the age of miracles is past.

XIX.—" A LITTLE KNOWLEDGE IS A DANGEROUS THING."

We reprint a paragraph from *The Manchester Courier*. It runs as follows :—

"The next gold rush is likely to take place in South Australia, the West Australian 'Boom' already showing signs of exhaustion. Much will depend upon the report of the Wennecke expedition, which started a few weeks back with the object of exploring the McDonnel range, lying near the centre of the continent. It will not return till the end of September or thereabouts, and meanwhile matters are pretty quiet, though a few prospecting parties are said to have proceeded north-ward. The South Australians are firmly convinced that they have paying gold reefs in that Colony, and they are said to exist besides in districts fairly accessible to transport, and with a far better water supply than the West Australian fields. The districts in everyone's mouth are those of Mount Pleasant, Blumberg, Waukaringa, and Nellinghoo. It must be confessed that the modest output of 15 dwts. per ton from a Blumberg reef hardly encourages extravagant hopes, especially as the other reefs have not been worked at all. However, we shall be a good deal wiser some six months hence."

Our contemporary appears to have a gift of prophecy which we do not pretend to, although we have made Australian goldmining a special study for many years. We have no objection whatever to their remark that

South Australia is to be the object of the next gold-rush, but we certainly take exception to the statement that "the West Australian Boom is already showing signs of exhaustion." In the first place we do not think that the American expression "Boom" is applicable to West Australia. The Westralians have never been given to that sort of thing. If they had a fault it is entirely in an opposite direction; for they have been modest and retiring from the very first; too prone indeed to "hide their light under a bushel." Again, the colony shows no sign whatever of exhaustion. Quite the contrary. We believe that the gold discoveries have scarcely well begun. We look forward to seeing every field, from Kimberley, in the North, to Dundas, in the South, in full swing. Does our contemporary for a moment imagine that the mere handful of miners and prospectors, who have turned their attention to Australia, have made a complete investigation of the gold-fields of Western Australia? Why, Kimberley alone is much larger in area than either Scotland or Ireland, and almost as large as England—the latter measuring 50,823, and the gold-fields 4,700 square miles We wish South Australia all success in her search for gold, and we hope that the Wennecke expedition will bring back golden tidings, both literally and figuratively. The colony is our next neighbour, if we may be allowed to speak from a Westralian point of view, and we can scarcely fail to share in her good luck, if such befall her, just as she is bound to participate in ours

Our contemporary tell us that the water supply is far better than on the West Australian fields. This observation is so extremely indefinite that it carries little force or meaning. Doubtless there are some districts in South Australia ; but the converse holds good, and *we can point to West Australian fields more bounteously supplied with both timber and water than some of the more arid and sterile tracts of South Australia.*

The *Courier's* concluding sentences are instructive, and almost seem to contradict the unfavourable prognostications and contemptuous tone in which they have opened fire on our youngest colony. "It must be confessed that the modest output of 15 dwts per ton from a Blumberg reef hardly encourages extravagant hopes (regarding South Australia), especially as the other reefs have not been worked at all. However, we shall be a good deal wiser some six months hence." Regarding this last statement, we can only hope that such will be the case. Before committing itself to such statements it would be well if our contemporary looked a little more closely into the facts of the case.

Perhaps the writer of the paragraph in question never even heard of Pilbarra gold-field, and yet it is larger than Scotland, and almost exactly the area of Ireland. From this field we print four cablegrams regarding three very important mines, two from the Mallina district, and two from the Marble Bar. In all these "The modest output of 15 dwts from a Blumberg reef" are far out distanced ; and these cablegrams we submit go far to disprove the somewhat incautious, and certainly unsupported assertion, that West Australian mining is showing signs of exhaustion.

XX.—A BAD CARVER HELPS NOBODY WELL.

The Carnarvon correspondent of the *West Australian,* "J.R.," who in the issue of 26th June last advocates the sub-division of Western Australia, is not exactly a heaven - born reformer. To start with, he assumes too much. He tells us that "a casual glance at the map, and a casual glimpse of the past history of Western Australia, must convince the thoughtful that Western Australia, with its 980,000 square miles of territory, is much too unwieldy to be governed from any one particular spot, be it Albany, Perth, Geraldton or Roebourne." Now a casual glance at the map, with the accompanying casual glimpse at colonial history, fail to carry conviction home to us, so we cannot be on the category of "the thoughtful" from "J.R.'s" point of view. We therefore will take a casual glance through his letter, in the hope of being further enlightened on the subject. "So vastly different are the conditions of the people, we are told, that no code of laws can be equally and equitably applicable to the whole." But this remark, alas! applies to every community. Law cannot be invariably Justice, and surely the vast difference which exists, according to the writer, among the handful of people who inhabit West Australia are as nothing compared with the differences which exist in nations outnumbering them by thousands to one.

"J.R.'s" remedy is to divide the colony up. Cut into three parts, and presumably, a separate code of laws for each part; he fancies everything would go smoothly. He anticipates one difficulty, and admits that separation in byegone days caused "endless bickering and ill-feeling; but in these present days of enlightenment we are informed the matter is approached in a friendly manner, and discussed most amicably by the parties concerned." This is certainly not our experience, and "bickering and ill-feeling" very feebly describes the accompaniments of attempted separation on this side of the globe. The Carnarvon reformer thus pays a high tribute of praise to the good intentions of Sir John Forrest and his mainstays. They have, it seems, "yearning desires" for the prosperity of the colony, but, "they might as well try to govern the planet Mars from the earth, as for Perth to govern West Australia." After having thus soared into the regions of hyperbole, whence we are unable to follow him, "J.R." proceeds to unfold his two schemes, under either of which the colony would make "rapid, onward stride in the march of progress."

His first plan is to "create out of one colony three distinct colonies; that is colonies with powers co-equal with the powers of the now existing colonies, with a Governor and a Representative Government." The southern division is to be re-named "South-Western Australia," the middle slice, "Western Australia," and the northern portion "Kingsland." "South Western Australia is to comprise that portion of the Australian

Continent extending from the parallel of 35 degrees 8 minutes south latitude, to the 29th degree of south latitude, and from the South Australian border to the Indian Ocean. It must be admitted that "J.R." has been remarkably liberal to this southern section. So far as we can see, by a casual glance, it would include every important town except Geraldton, the chief seaports, three goldfields, not to mention nine tenths of the population. It would lose its distinctive name of "Western Australia," however, which title is reserved for the centre division, inhabited, be it observed, by no less a personage than "J.R." himself. It seems a pity that this gentleman did not happen to pitch his tent further south; but he makes the best of it, and apportions a huge territory, extending over 9 degrees to "Western Australia," under the new system. Murchison, Ashburton and Pilbarra gold-fields are included in this middle cut, and the inhabitants of this enormous area, which is about as large as Great Britain and Ireland, France and Germany combined, would muster five or six thousand souls. No doubt, however, this modern edition of Pope Alexander VI., whose division of the world made him renowned among the Pontiffs, would gladly undertake the Governorship of this mammoth colony, and frame a suitable code of laws.

Were "Kingsland,"—as the northern colony is to be called—not so conspicuously torrid, we should have been disposed to say she had been left out in the cold." We are given no hint as to the derivation of the name. We certainly have a northern suburb of London called

"Kingsland," but this probably never occurred to "J.R." However, this tropical colony is to comprise all that portion of the Australian continent from the parallel of the 20th degree of south latitude to the northernmost portion of Australia, and from the 139th degree of longitude to the Indian Ocean. Being very much smaller than the other two colonies "J.R.," it will be noted, cuts off no less than 10 degrees from South Australia.

To sum up his first scheme, we have the South Western colony (or "Westralia" for preference, remarks this master of alternatives) "distinctly agricultural and mining; 'Western Australia' pastoral and mining, and 'Kingsland' being tropical." This would-be reformer, after prophesying great, grand, and glorious results, expresses a natural doubt as to whether the different colonies "would be able to support a Government with its attendant paraphernalia." This difficulty certainly occurred to us. "Kingsland," for example, would be about as large as England and France, with some thirteen hundred inhabitants, a great many being natives and Malay pearl-fishers; and "West Australia," in spite of having the inventor of the scheme on the spot, would encounter practical obstacles in administering her new code. Doubtless Carnarvon would be chosen as the seat of Government, being central; the distance from, say Cossack to Geraldton, puts the latter place out of the question.

Before describing his second scheme, in case the first misses fire, which is not improbable, "J.R." takes us into his confidence. He is a strong Home Ruler it seems, and he tells us that Ireland will ultimately be "governed by Irish notions, by Irish prejudices, and by Irish patriotism." He waxes so eloquent on this subject that he almost forgets to enlighten us on his second scheme, which is shortly a head Government with two subordinate Governments, and these two would be divided into three States each. "It matters not," he says, how many portions Australia is divided into, she is Australia still." This is evidently the principle upon which "J.R." works, but we fail to see the advantage to be derived. You may turn Western Australia into "The United States of Westralia," or adopt "J.R.'s" lopsided system of subdivision, but it would be well to wait until she has arrived at a more advanced stage of development, and possesses a population capable of such adjustments. In two of the colonies, as proposed by this person, there would be about one inhabitant to each 150 square miles. This would be even a worse and more unmanageable state of things than the present, which gives a result of about 18 individuals per square mile.

Our readers may be interested in reading of a scheme promulgated half a century ago, reprinted from *Simmond's Colonial Magazine* for August, 1845. It will be noted that the sanguine writer expected that the whole continent would be over run and settled by 1865.

From *Simmond's Colonial Magazine*, August, 1845:

"Port Phillip should be at once separated from New South Wales, and have an independent Government of her own. They are much too far apart, and their interests are too distinct for them ever to work well together. Indeed there is quite space enough for the establishment of another independent territory or state between them. Portland Bay should also be called into a separate existence, limited by the line that now separates it from South Australia, between which and Western Australia there is sufficient room for two other Governments. The east coast is extending from New South Wales through Moreton Bay, and other settlements to the northward, and will no doubt continue round in that direction to the Gulf of Carpentaria. The western settlements can be continued on that side till they meet. The centre of the country will at some time or other be explored and settled, until, as we now do everything at railway speed, in some twenty years the whole continent will be over run and settled."

XXI.—BAYLEY'S AT LAST FINDS A RIVAL.

Of many people it may be said that, although open to conviction, it is extremely hard to convince them. This has been our painful experience on many occasions, but never more so than when we have strenuously asserted that the great mine of stupendous wealth at Coolgardie, known as "Bayley's Reward," was not the *rara avis in terris*, the prodigy, the phenomenon, the exception, which many would have us believe. That the claim was exceptionally rich no one will deny; but that nature had put all her gold into one purse, and dropped it into Bayley's "pocket," we considered an absurd idea. According to the ordinary doctrine of probabilities, the notion that this mine was unique, solitary, alone in its golden grandeur, was incredible. Supposing, for the sake of argument, it was the mine *par excellence*, the richest reef on the Yilgarn Field, which it may be stated is larger than Scotland, and just about equal in area to Ireland. The "Reward Claim" consisted of a five acre block, through which a reef ran. Now, is it within the range of possibility that two men could, after a few weeks search, hit upon the right spot in such an immense territory? A needle in a haystack would be in comparison quite easy to find, or a sixpence buried in a twenty acre field.

But the Coolgardie neighbourhood gave every indication of auriferous wealth, and it seemed ridiculous to argue that because one big fish had been caught nothing but small fry could be expected thereafter. Yet, such were the statements made again and again, all to the effect that Nature, having been prodigal in one locality, would be found to have drained all the surrounding districts of gold, and left them poor indeed. We think that these views were chiefly promulgated by the apostles of caution, who never saw a goldfield in their lives, but, adopting the tactics of pessimism and detraction, are constantly on the watch for some mishap, so as to be ready to cry out, "*I told you so.*" Mere force of reason and ordinary common sense operates but slowly, if it operates at all, upon such creatures; but Gold is a wonderful clearer of the understanding. It seems to dissipate doubts and scruples as if by magic, and convinces the most obstinate. And so the *rara avis* theory has been effectually exploded by recent news from Coolgardie. First we have the marvellous discovery, by the lucky half-dozen of weary and disheartened miners, who by a happy chance lighted on the Londonderry Reef. Someone has said it is better to be born lucky than rich, but here is an agreeable combination of the two attributes. We learn that two of the six, however, have sold their respective shares for £3,000 each, and we fancy Messrs. Dawson and Carter—the gentlemen in question—must be rather sorry for themselves, if, as is stated, Mr Begelhole has been able to pay £50,000 cash and a sixth interest for the mine. The purchaser has made a good bargain, moreover, if the yield is as reported. From Perth, on July 3rd, Mr. Scantlebury, of Sydney, a would-be purchaser, states that dollying operations are furnishing 1,000 ozs. of gold per day. At this rate, about a fortnight would enable Mr. Begelhole to recoup himself. We refrain from commenting upon this output until we have fuller particulars.

Small wonder indeed that we read of wild excitement, "febrile in its intensity," as the correspondent of the *Perth Daily News* puts it, in pathologic phrase. Certain contradictions, exaggerations and inaccuracies are inevitable under such circumstances; the fever alone would account for them. For example: one account tells us that the "reef is of ironstone formation, and of glassy nature;" while another states that "the ironstone, with which reef gold is usually associated when met with in large quantities, is entirely absent. The gold is carried in a clear quartz of a slightly amber colour." These, however, are minor details, the main point being established that a great discovery of gold has been made.

We had scarcely recovered from the surprise occasioned by Londonderry tidings, when we received an additional shock, through the medium of Reuter's cable. Another astounding discovery has come to light, at about 50 miles distance from the claim referred to, or about 40 miles north of Coolgardie, probably, so far as we can judge, somewhere about ten miles south of Black Flag Mine. The finder is said to be an agent of a Perth Syndicate. Four hundredweight of specimens were brought into the local branch of the Union Bank of Australia, and were personally inspected by the Warden, who estimates the gold as more than the weight of stone

—that is, roughly speaking, worth about £10,000. We cannot think that the Warden would be guilty of wilful exaggeration, although he may be wrong in his estimate; if so, however, the specimens may be even more valuable than he asserts. We shall anxiously wait for further particulars of this latest find, which, coming on the top of the Londonderry Bonanza, is almost bewildering. A mining expert said, at the Coolgardie banquet given to the Premier last month, that the district would take years of prospecting to lay bare its riches, and that there were dozens of "Bayley's Reward" in the field. Since Bayley and Ford's discovery, no West Australian field has been more skilfully and assiduously explored than Coolgardie, although by a mere handful of miners, in comparison with its great extent. These few men, however, have produced results which clearly demonstrate the auriferous wealth of this goldfield. From the above facts, then, we are finally led to the conclusion that on Coolgardie there are many rich reefs awaiting discovery; and if such be the case regarding Coolgardie, the same may be said of each and every field already declared throughout the length and breadth of the Colony. Nay, we may go further, and say that even the declared gold fields themselves may not prove eventually to be the richest districts; for at some unsuspected locality may be auriferous treasures utterly eclipsing anything already brought to light. A leading article in the *Daily Telegraph*, of August 10th, referring to the Londonderry mine, contains these words:—" For many years past those best acquainted with the resources of Western

Australia have been prophesying a brilliant future for that colony." A prophet is said to have little honour in his own country, and certainly, like Cassandra of old, he gains precious little credence. This may have been the case with us, but we certainly have all along foretold the coming greatness of Westralia's gold-fields, and assured, like Priam's daughter, we spoke truly. When the other fields are placed on the par with Coolgardie in respect of roads, railways, telegraph lines, capital, skill, men, and world-wide advertisement, we venture to predict such revelations from Murchison, Pilbarra, Kimberley, Ashburton, and other undeclared parts of the colony as will make all the world wonder; and award Western Australia the palm as the greatest of gold producing countries. She has been well named the "Coming Colony," and "Coming events cast their shadows before." Her gold is indeed " As the shadow of a great rock in a weary land."

XXII.—SWEAR NOT AT ALL.

We are concerned to learn, through a somewhat lengthy correspondence in the column of a contemporary, that "bad language" is extremely prevalent in Western Australia, and on the increase. It is a curious idiom, by the way, which makes this expression a synonym for profanity, indecency, and the like, and which in short makes "bad language" a wicked accomplishment, while "Bad English" or "Bad grammar" are not incompatible with piety and goodness of the first water. "Cornelia" says she has been all over the world, and to the other Australian colonies, but never were her ears so offended as in West Australia. "Saxon" expresses very fully his horror at the blasphemy, coupled with the use of the 'universal adjective," in the streets of Perth, which is not confined to men, but extends to young lads, and even to members of the fair sex. "Let me say," the writer continues, "that it is only since the prosperity of Western Australia has opened her ports to persons from the other Australian colonies and England that we have heard so much of this bad language." We are likewise told that on the Yilgarn field nineteen men out of twenty curse and swear appallingly; but "Saxon" has made the discovery that nineteen out of twenty are "T'othersiders" or Britishers, which he remarks "is significant." Another correspondent, who signs himself very appropriately "D——," does not so much object to the foul language itself as to its dull uniformity. Its adjectival and rhetorical sameness palls on his ear, and he holds up, as an example for imitation, Shakespeare's soldier, who was "full of *strange* oath." All this person wants is artistic profanity, and suggests the importation of original expression!

There can be no question as to the demoralizing and degrading influence which habitual bad language exercise over a community, and this is specially shown by the class of men and women who use it on all occasions. In England, they either as a rule belong to the very lowest stratum of society, or to the professionally vicious and criminal classes, so far as both sexes are concerned. Racing men and gamblers are specially addicted to the vice, and throughout all classes of society it must be confessed, that if not exactly "bad," at least strong language is on occasions indulged in. We quite understand the sort of abominable manner of speech which the Perth correspondents allude to. It is the constant interlarding of ordinary conversation with certain coarse and senseless words and phrases, so very common in the United States. In America the "universal adjective," which we take to be a synonym for "sanguinary," is not used however. Originally this was not an adjective at all, but an oath—to wit "By Our Lady." This became "By'r lady," and eventually "Gory!" The gentleman who objects to sameness will be glad to hear that the old adjectival form has for the most part been abandoned, in "artistic" circles, for the present participle of the verb " to bleed," which is considered more graphic and picturesque. We have already stated that gamblers are frequently swearers, no doubt finding considerable relief in the practice when in bad luck. Possibly this may account for the majority at Yilgarn, and we can almost excuse a certain amount of expletive on the goldfields. In Scotland swearing has always been treated with a certain tenderness, being considered a grand set off to the conversation. "It's a pity swearing's such a sin," said an old Caledonian lady, "it much such a man of our Jock." She may likewise have been responsible for the following Sabbatarian household rule :—"Swearing's bad, drinking not much better; but whistling on the Lord's day I will not permit."

A few words are unfortunate enough to sound like profane language, which are innocent enough. "I don't care a *dam*" is the correct spelling of a familiar expression. The "dam" is a small Indian coin, worth a fraction of a farthing; and we are told in the Koran that when the husband is absent from home the good wife will be careful and not spend a *dam* more than necessary. "I don't care a *rapp*" is commonly used; and the "rapp" is an infinitesmally small Swiss coin. Space forbids our dilating further on the curiosities of "cuss-language," and we content ourselves with a fervent hope that the Westralians may not meet with such bad luck as will tempt them to swear, and that if they encounter good fortune they may not advertise the fact by pyrotechnic display of profanity. In either case it is, to say the least of it, stupid.

XXIII.—ON 'JUMPERS' AND THEIR WICKED WAYS.

There is no section of the Western Australian Mining Laws and Regulations more in need of revision and alteration than that which relates to "Jumpers." It would appear that in a new country this individual is recognized as a necessary evil of the gold-fields. Without his watchful vigilance the mines would be swallowed up by monopolists. The knowledge that jumping will ensue, if the labour conditions are not complied with, keeps the field in wholesome running order. The "jumper" may in a measure be likened to certain vermin which invade the persons and homes of those who neglect cleanliness, and in that sense necessary evils, however, obnoxious. Indeed one variety can certainly claim to be the greatest "jumpers" in the animal world, far surpassing Mark Twain's Jumping Frog.

There are several species of the genus "jumper" in the mining world. First, the casual or occasional "jumper," who knocking about on prospecting, or any honest labour bent, notices that a certain unoccupied claim is liable to forfeiture. He thereupon exercises his right, and applies for possession. This stamp of "jumper" cannot be objected to, and it was for him and his like that the law was enacted.

There is, however, the professional "jumper," who, most of all resembles the lively familiar insect, inasmuch as he does little else but jump. They do nothing whatever to develop the district which they infest, and are for the most part a common nuisance. To fatten on the labours of others is the aim and object of their unworthy lives. Sometimes they will extort black-mail, under threats of continuing the application for forfeiture of a claim, or failing this, they will endeavour to sell the property for their own benefit. Any enactment which may frustrate their plans, and so banish these plagues of the goldfields, will be both acceptable and welcome. A third class are the so-called " friendly jumpers," who in spite of their amicable title, must be admitted to be the most dangerous kind of all. Their action simply nullifies the law, and enables a mine owner to suspend work with impunity. Being in collusion with the proprietor, the two work in partnership to evade the mining conditions, and it is of course a matter of difficulty to deal with such cases. It has been suggested that if jumped property were not handed to the " jumper," but put up to auction,—the " jumper " receiving a proportion of the price—(just as the common informer some time receives a proportion of the fine) collusion would be nipped in the bud. In any case it is to be hoped that some method may be adopted for mitigating the evil. The mining laws and regulations require a thorough overhauling; and we cannot but think that the colonial equivalent of a Royal Commission, with power of examining witnesses, should be appointed in Western Australia. Expert and practical local evidence should be taken from each of the gold-fields, and the regulations, if necessary, modified to suit each individual district. Western Australia owes her present celebrity to her goldfield, and she should spare no effort to secure a wise and comprehensive code of laws applying thereto.

XXIV.—THE GOVERNMENT AND THE WATER QUESTION.

Australia is, in some respects, a land of contraries. Western Australia gave curious effect to the words of Juvenal, "Rara avis in terris nigroque simillima cygno," when the black swan of fable was found to be a reality. Her bear is a harmless beast, and her kangaroo an oddity. Another peculiarity of the colony is that instead of "laying by for a rainy day," she has to save up for a dry day. Drought has been her *bête noir*, the thorn in her side, or, as Sir Malcolm Fraser calls it, the skeleton in the cupboard. Coolgardie—richest in gold—has been poorest in water; but, being wealthy, her cry for relief has been listened to and acted upon. Let us hope that the works which have been accomplished may fully attain their object.

It is generally admitted that the quantity of rain which falls from one season to another would prove sufficient for all useful purposes if the rainfall were properly husbanded. Hitherto, however, only limited success has attended the efforts of Government and private enterprise to deal with the question of water supply on the Western Australian goldfields. The more distant areas of Kimberley, Pilbarra and Murchison, although from time to time sorely perplexed through drought in different places, never seem to have been in such a waterless plight as Yilgarn. After Coolgardie was discovered, it was found that the further prospectors penetrated into the desert the greater was the scarcity of water, until the sufferings undergone by mining pioneers became intolerable, hundreds having to leave the field, which threatened to become a Valley of Death. Two years ago from 6d. up to 5s. a gallon was paid for water, which had to be carted many miles. Bayley, Hannan, Cashman and others having demonstrated beyond dispute the great wealth of the district, the Government began to move in the direction of remedying this terrible evil. Two dams were constructed at Coolgardie, each with a holding capacity of something less than a million gallons. This sounded well for a start, but unfortunately we soon afterwards learnt that one of them was comparatively useless. It was constructed, it seems, on a perfectly flat country, with no water shed except that formed by the artificial channels leading to it. At this period, we understand, a bore was put down about two hundred feet, and though water was struck, rising to over 30 ft. in the bore, work was suddenly suspended and nothing further done.

Mr. Renou, the Superintendent of Water Supply, inspected the gold-fields, and submitted a voluminous report, and among other things recommended the utilization of the lake at Southern Cross, by excavations, for the supply of the principal mines in the neighbourhood; showing that this could be done with comparative ease and economy. The total capacity of the dam and tank he estimated at between 80 and 90 million gallons, and the cost about £8,000. Instead of having suitable provision against drought, Southern Cross had but three underground tanks of very limited capacity, one of which, holding 10,000 gallons, belonged to the Government. The road to Coolgardie was also inspected, and found sadly deficient. Various points were marked out where it was essential to have tanks of considerable capacity. Natural water-courses or permanent surface waters there were, none for hundreds of miles all round.

It is obvious that such a state of affairs loudly demanded the immediate and energetic attention of the authorities, and it would appear that since last year considerable work has been carried out between Southern Cross and Coolgardie. The Premier is very sanguine as to the future, so far as an adequate water supply in this quarter is concerned. "The work has been well done," he says. "Not only is it sufficient, but it has been splendidly performed. There is no danger of the traffic being stopped between Coolgardie and the Cross. As soon as rain comes the water difficulty along the road will have disappeared, and, I think, for ever." And then Sir John Forrest goes on to describe the gargantuan allowance of water which is to be at the wayfarer's disposal. The gist of his statements was set forth in our last issue.

Mr. Jobson is the Moses of the district, according to one speaker at the Coolgardie banquet to the Premier, and this gentleman will have earned the gratitude of as many men as there were Israelites in the wilderness, if he has solved the water problem. Jupiter Pluvius will no doubt perform his part in due season, and the dragon will at last be slain which has guarded the golden apples of the Australian Hesperides.

Regarding the probability of finding an artesian supply, Sir John Forrest said that there was "no reason why deep sinking should not be tried." The Kauffman borer was to be brought from Southern Cross, being "cheaper and more suitable than the diamond drill," which, according to the Premier, has never been used in any part of Australia for deep sinking for water. We are not prepared to dispute this statement, and have every reason to believe that the Kauffman is an excellent borer in spite of its failure at Southern Cross. "From an economical point of view," concludes the Premier, "the Kauffman is superior to the diamond drill." If anyone less capable of judging the question had reiterated the point of cheapness regarding this apparatus, we should have been disposed to urge that money should be a secondary object were the chance of obtaining artesian water was concerned. Such an achievement would do much to revolutionize many parts of the colony. As Mr. Henty, in his Address-in-Reply at the opening of Parliament, said "In the north there are immense tracts of fertile land undeveloped for want of water, and the same applies to the pastoral and agricultural industries, as well as to the goldfields. If we had an artesian well successfully put down, the colony would have a new impetus, and we would have increased settlement." These sentiments were expressed in the Legislative Council; and in the Legislative Assembly, Mr. Wood's Address-in-Reply contained the following:—"I hope to see a distinct effort made in search of an artesian supply, both on the goldfield and in the Nor'-West, where, owing to an uncertain rainfall, a large expenditure would be justified in order to avert, if possible, the disastrous effects of the too frequent droughts experienced in that part of the colony." Mr. Hardy likewise endorsed this view, and Mr. Burges went so far as to accuse the Government of having neglected their duty.

It can scarcely be, that because the Government geologist has declared that artesian water will not be found in the Yilgarn district that so few efforts have been made to find it elsewhere.

We hope, in any case, that the authorities will now give special prominence to the water question. It is not enough to have tanks, bores, wells, soaks and so forth laid down on paper, or gallons of water merely represented by rows of figures. Statistics are proverbially *dry*, and the gold miners and travellers must have something that will quench their thirst and sustain life, to say nothing of domestic and steam purposes. The Government has certainly the mandate of the people to set this "burning" question at rest throughout the goldfields and the colony generally. The voice crying in the wilderness has too long cried in vain.

XXV.—SIEGE OF LONDONDERRY. HUXLEY'S DEFENCE.

A celebrated Lord Chancellor, in advising a friend against embarking in litigation, is reported to have said: "If a man asked me for my coat, and I thought he was serious in his demand, I would rather give him my coat and my waistcoat, too, than go to law about it." No doubt, having witnessed the long drawn agonies of so many tortured litigants, his lordship was inclined to speak strongly, and if a coat only was the bone of contention his advice was sound enough. Nevertheless, we can scarcely blame a party of exceptionally lucky gold-diggers who, having a mine of proved wealth at their backs, are striving to retain possession of a neighbouring claim which, but for a certain regulation, would have been their undoubted property.

The line of defence taken in the case of Lyon and Huxley, popularly known as "The Londonderry Jumping Case," was bold and ingenious. The defendant is one of the lucky discoverers of the Londonderry reef, and is applicant for a gold mining lease immediately adjacent to the original find; while the plaintiff seeks to have this application declared forfeited; for, among other things, the non-fulfilment of the labour conditions imposed by regulation sixty-two under the Goldfields Act.

The defence is two-fold, and raises two questions.

(1.) Whether an applicant, during the pendency of his application has a right which is forfeitable at the suit of an individual.

(2.) Whether the regulation under the Gold Fields Act, enforcing the labour conditions, is *ultra vires* the Statute. It will be seen that if the first question should be answered in the negative, the plaintiff's case would fall to the ground, for the very evident reason that if no forfeitable right existed during pendency of application, it would be impossible to forfeit a non-existent right. If on the other hand the second question were answered in the affirmative, the regulation itself is impugned and may be rejected altogether.

The Warden, Mr. Finnerty—very naturally, we think, —stood by the regulation, statute or no statute; and he likewise decided that the applicant has an estate on interest in the ground which is liable to forfeiture for non-compliance with the regulation. We could scarcely have expected the Warden to come to any other conclusion; however able may have been the arguments of the defendant. He had the regulations before him, evidently framed for the express purpose of dealing with certain cases.

Such a case presented itself, and it would have been almost tantamount to an expression of opinion that the Government conveyancers did not know their business, to have done otherwise than given his judgment on the bare letter of the regulation.

Nevertheless, while quite comprehending the Warden's action, and fully admitting his right to hold by the validity of the regulations, we can scarcely understand his refusal to grant a special case on the point, so that the question which is one of law, pure and simple, might be argued before the judges of the Supreme Court, and finally decided. As a matter of fact, this opportunity is lost, and we shall very probably have the same defence and contention brought up again and again until decided. This seems to have been a legitimate case of "Jumping," and one which gained general sympathy, but it is to be regretted that the Huxley defence seems to complicate an already complicated and troublesome operation, namely, dealing with, and legislating for "Jumpers."

As to the forensic aspect of the case, we shall not attempt to discuss its merits. The Statute, we know, is paramount, and unless regulations are framed under its sanction, Mr. Huxley might sing with the Grand Duchess of Gerolstein, "Hang the Regulation." The Warden, having recommended the Minister of Crown Lands to grant the forfeiture, it is probable it will be granted. At the same time, however, it is very possible that the matter may be submitted for consideration to the law officer of the Crown. We can only hope that whatever decision is arrived at may tend to simplify the regulations and expedite procedure upon the Goldfields.

XXVI.—PROSPECTING AGAIN REWARDED.

The details of the last great gold discovery, forty miles from Coolgardie, which are contained in another page, fully realise the expectations raised by the cablegram which announced the fact a few weeks ago. The recurrence of these great natural hoards of gold touch very deeply the interests of Western Australia. As yet we have only the barest inkling of her capabilities. Many years must elapse before these can be fully tested, her population being so utterly inadequate, and disproportionate to her vast bulk. Her people have nevertheless done wonders; and are at present doing the two best things possible for the country, viz :—constructing railways, and making provisions for rainless seasons and waterless districts, so that her territories may become accessible, and the traveller across her roads may be enabled to reach the most distant goldfields with a certain degree of safety and comfort.

There will, however, for many years to come be regions throughout her immense expanse which will attract the explorer, prospector, or pioneer-squatter beyond the ken of road or railway, and far remote from civilization. Thousands of square miles lie within the boundaries of the colony which have never yet been trodden by European foot. In a sense, of course, the country may be said to have been explored. The theory of a vast inland lake, or a river equal in size to the Amazon draining the whole breadth of Australia, has been exploded. Such brave men as Eyre, Gregory, Forrest, Giles and others have fought their way across the deserts. We see their tracks marked on the map, and read accounts of their expeditions. But the line which marks their progress, slender as it is on paper, would measure many miles in width by the scale of the largest chart; in fact no mark visible to the naked eye would truly indicate their line of travel. They, therefore, saw but little of the country on their march. Moreover their journeys were too long to admit of more than a mere general examination of the regions through which they passed—minute and special investigations being left to others. In 1856, for example, Gregory passed through a section of the present Kimberley Goldfield; in 1873, Colonel Warburton was on Pilbarra; three years later Giles traversed Ashburton, having the previous season skirted Yilgarn; and yet none of the explorers found gold. The reason is clear. They had other objects in view, and since they made no search for the precious metal, unless some chance circumstance forced it on their view, it was unlikely that they would discover it. Now that it has been found, however, *gold* is the main object of the prospecting explorer. The *fauna* and *flora* are of very small moment to such men as Bayley, the Londonderry sextette, or "Honest John" Dunn, the latest hero of the hour. Such men as Sir Joseph Banks, it will be said, possessed the gold already, or they would not have been so eager for portfolios full of dried specimens, or stuffed birds and native weapons. Truly the Wealth of Nations Syndicate is to be congratulated.

It is pleasant to hear of some of the good luck falling to the lot of men who have been born and bred in the colony. Still the West Australians do not grudge the slices of good fortune which have fallen to the lot of Victorians, South Australians, Queenslanders and others; they are all Australians after all.

And should an occasional Britisher light on a golden reef, it may well be said that we all acknowledge allegiance to the same gracious Lady whose effigy adorns our coinage. Nay, if even a miner from the Great Republic should "strike it rich," he speaks the same language, as ourselves, and we have learnt an occasional wrinkle from Uncle Sam. The only human being with whom the West Australian refuses to share his wealth is the Asiatic. The Chinaman may grow vegetables, peddle tea, or iron shirts and collars, but he must leave the gold reefs alone. The mines are the property of the Government under the Crown, and they are fully satisfied in leasing them only to those who will contribute to the building up of a nation. For such a purpose the Asiatic is useless.

We note that Mr. A. Forrest was at a Military Ball in Perth, when the news of the great find came to the capital. We are naturally reminded of the Duchess of Richmond's Ball at Brussels on the night of the 17th June, 1815, regarding which Byron sings:

> "There was a sound of revelry by night,
> "And Belgium's capital had gathered there,
> "Her beauty and her chivalry."

Mr. Forrest left the ball-room, bound for Coolgardie;

Wellington did likewise *en route* for Waterloo. We can only hope that the mine will carry out the abundantly rich promise with which it starts.

During the past week, by far the most active business in the African market in the Stock Exchange has been associated with Western Australian shares. This fact has been promptly noted by the *Financial Times*, and as there is every prospect of that arena of mining enterprise continuing to absorb a large proportion, if not the preponderance of the public attention devoted to mines, our up-to-date contemporary feels that the time for a revision of nomenclature has arrived, and however members of the Stock Exchange may prefer adherence to usage, they decline to regard a section of the Antipodes as part of South Africa, even a market sense. "African and West Australian Market" appears a more suitable designation, under the new condition of things, and that heading now appears in the column of the paper. The same authority considers that the persistent tendency of mining shares to gravitate to what has still been called the South African market is partly because that section embraces more capital and enterprise, and also because "scalping" proclivities are not pursued to such an intolerable extent as in the other department.

XXVII.—WESTERN AUSTRALIA'S CHIEF NEED: POPULATION.

The aboriginal of Western Australia is rather a selfish person where food is concerned. As a rule he has to go out and catch his dinner before he has the opportunity of cooking it, which is appetising work. When therefore he has captured and roasted his kangaroo or wild turkey, or collected and prepared his dish of frogs, fish, or edible grubs, his hunger is apt to overcome his hospitality, which does not usually extend beyond his family circle. There is one great occasion, however, when he becomes most friendly, and his heart expands to such an extent that he desires the company of all and sundry. This overflow of goodfellowship and milk of human kindness occurs when he discovers a stranded whale. It is the aboriginal equivalent of a 'Welcome Nugget' or 'Bayley's Reward.' Such a huge outcropping reef of solid meat cannot be worked single-handed, so he lights bonfires, which is the native way of issuing prospectuses; and very soon he forms a company who fall to with a will, and gorge for a few weeks, carrying away with them evil-smelling chunks to their absent friends.

It is a universal law, and a wise one, which dictates to men that where they have barely enough for their own support they should not invite others to aggravate their poverty. The principle benefits the excluded as well as the excluders, and it is therefore to be commended.

Hitherto the white population of Western Australia

have been constrained to act somewhat on the aboriginal system, and have been slow to encourage immigration. Possibly the miseries endured for a while, shortly after the Swan River Settlement was initiated by Captain Stirling, has left a strain of extra caution on their blood. West Australia was so far away, so ungainly in size, and her people troubled themselves so little to advertise her good qualities so far as they had discovered them, that she attracted but few emigrants from the United Kingdom. It must be remembered, for example, that Sydney in 1829, contained as many inhabitants as Perth does at the present time. Then again the sister colonies were all in turn discovered to be auriferous, and seemed to offer more advantages to the settler than the western dependency. Indeed the attacks of gold fever, with which the neighbouring territories were in turn attacked, caused many to leave Western Australia never to return. Her early history was exceptionally unfortunate.

We were rather struck the other day to see in an old book on the Colonies, written in 1829, the following remark—"On the first rumour (in 1828) of a colony being formed at Swan River, I inserted at the venture the Latin name of London—*Londinium*—merely as a suggestion, there being no place of this name in the world. The public are aware that a town is marked out twelve miles up the Swan River and named Perth, a name, by the way, that will attract precious few emigrants, there being a great deal in a name." The writer turned out to be a true prophet. Only the other day Sir Malcolm Fraser gave a somewhat guarded reply to the *Central News* representative on the subject of emigration. Apparently the Colony wants immigrants of the right sort only. Having had experience of the very wrong sort—the prisoners of the Crown—Western Australia would feign be more fastidious in the future. But the convicts, in many respects, benefited the Colony, and we have been rather disposed to deprecate the language of exclusiveness in which all invitation to emigrants has been couched. West Australia *must* have population, and she cannot afford to be over particular. The *Western Mail* says, in a recent article, "The mother country has hitherto sent us very few men and women whom she can spare, and for whom we have ample room. To Great Britain we look, not merely for the money, but for men." We are gratified to note that through her press Western Australia is now inviting men and women to share her good fortune. In this she unconsciously copies the original owners of the land, who could not bear to see the whale go to loss when there were hungry mouths to fill. We sincerely hope that a goodly contingent of England's sons and daughters will hearken and respond to the summons. We can well spare them. The Colonials, however, must be content with such as we *can* spare; no country likes to part with her very best. The main point to be observed is the pressing need for an increase of population, and it is to be hoped that with all her magnificent stores of wealth "in sight," that the Government will hold out every possible inducement for emigrants to seek her shores and develop her splendid resources.

The city editor of the *Pall Mall Gazette* has recently set a new fashion in West Australian mining criticism which has been followed by some of our contemporaries, and it is a fashion that does not at all become many of the companies upon which it has been fitted. Mr. J. Leslie Walker, who acknowledges the impartial tone which characterises the *Pall Mall's* remarks upon the various companies that are brought before the public, considers that they are in error in always comparing the acreage of a mine as regards the capital, instead of being guided by the length and richness of the reef or reefs that are upon the property. The appropriateness of this objection must be apparent to all who have read our contemporary's "city article" recently. If a large property is capitalised at £1,500 per acre, it is accepted as a fair priced one, whereas the £5,000 per acre, which was asked for "Blackett's Claim," was regarded in this quarter as too large. The mistake of this style of criticism is that the company promoters have not been slow to take advantage of it, and, instead of offering the public a small block of land at a certain figure, they reduce the price per acre by increasing the number of acres. In more than one case recently this trick has been resorted to, and promoters have increased their area by taking up an adjoining block of practically worthless land, and the whole property has been offered to the public at so much per acre all round. As we had occasion to remark in the case of the Empress of Coolgardie prospectus, the two claims which constituted the property, had an area of eighteen acres, and, while the smaller claim of six acres were reported upon and made much of, the claim of twelve acres was not enlarged upon, and we surmised it was secured as a site for the erection of machinery. Again, the *Pall Mall Gazette* always considers that £15,000 is much too little to be reserved as working capital. "As a general rule," Mr. Walker says, "this would be so in most mining enterprises, but does not apply to these Australian mines, owing to their richness, and the ease with which the quartz is reduced, requiring very few stamps. Bayley's Reward produced £80,000 without any stamps at all, and now only has ten stamps going." On this point we are more inclined to side with our contemporary than with Mr. Walker. Bayley's Reward, the Londonderry and the Wealth of Nations are doubtless easily worked, but they are exceptional cases, and they too, have had the water difficulty to contend with. With these Southern mines, the miner has generally one or two obstacles to contend with. At Coolgardie it is want of water; on the Murchison it is want of timber. It is seldom that both these vital necessities to gold mining are to be had in abundance in Western Australia, and these difficulties cost money to overcome. For all that the sum of £15,000 will in many cases prove sufficient for properly developing a W.A. property, provided (1) that the property is a good one, and (2) that it is under capable and economical management.

XXVIII.—ADVICE GRATIS IS APT TO BE WORTHLESS.

"In the multitude of counsellors there is safety," according to Solomon; but if we sought safety in the multitude of newspaper correspondents, who volunteer advice regarding West Australian mining matters, we should trust in a broken reed. Editors profess to accept no responsibility for the opinions of their correspondents; nevertheless, as far as possible, they steer clear of printing what Max O'Rell calls "tommy-rot." A good deal of arrant rubbish on the subject of West Australian mining has found its way into print, and gains a spurious credence from its presence in high-class journals. These letters for the most part reiterate the hackneyed advice, "Play for safety," in various forms. They are all gratuitous, and nearly all worthless, being hall-marked with the unmistakeable stamp of ignorance.

It is to be regretted that "Australia," who hails from Thames Ditton, did not think his letter to the *Pall Mall Gazette* worthy of his own signature, for then we should know what degree of importance to attach to it. He premises his following remarks, with the statement that he has spent *all his life in Western Australia*. From this we must perforce deduct such portion of his earthly pilgrimage as he has spent elsewhere—at Thames Ditton for instance. Having thus introduced himself, we are informed that a sense of duty impels him to sound such a note of warning as may perchance reach the *ears*—figuratively speaking—of the investing public.

His testimony as a life-long resident of the colony, with which the second paragraph of his epistle opens, is valuable. "I have no doubt," he says, "that Western Australia, as a gold-producing country, will prove equal in richness and permanency to any other of our colonies;" and then he goes on to warn the public against absolutely worthless claims. We are next introduced to a purely hypothetical property yielding 350 ounces to the ton by sample, and requiring £15,000 working capital. There would be, he thinks, ten or twenty tons of ore handy in such a mine (if the sample was a fair one) to enable the happy owners to dolly out by hand twenty or thirty thousand pounds worth of gold, without wasting their time looking for outside capital. This is very true, no doubt; but supposing the owners wished to sell their claim to a company as Bayley and Ford did, or as the Londonderry people did—surely they have a perfect right to do so, and make sure of their money. And in such cases the investing public reap the benefit, and share the good fortune of the finder who is foolish enough—or it may be wise enough—to accept an offer of cash down and a share in the concern, instead of hand-dollying all by himself. We suppose it will be said that the Wealth of Nations Syndicate should subscribe no money for machinery until they had knocked out enough gold by hand labour. This system might have been applicable to the Ophir mines, where Solomon procured his bullion.

Another point regarding the purchase of claims deserves attention. Supposing, for the sake of argument, that some toil-worn miners have struck such a Bonanza as "Australia" describes the Londonderry, for example; would it be natural or desirable that they should refuse every offer, and dolly out the gold they needed. We think not. Two of their number were thankful to get a couple of thousand pounds down, while the remaining quartette, wiser in their generation, were glad to pocket a good many thousands each, and be rid of the enormous responsibility, if not risk, of working such a mine on their own account. In short, the reason that high-class mines get into the market at all is that the discoverers are content with a sum which often constitutes great wealth in their eyes, and have that human preference for the bird in the hand which is worth two in the bush, and especially in the Australian bush.

Our correspondent next gives vent to a remarkable statement:—"I should like it to be understood that gold, in the gold-bearing fissure lodes, runs in shoots, varying say from twenty to one hundred feet wide." Now, however much "Australia" would "like this to be understood," we do think any person will readily understand it. Shoots of gold, twenty to one hundred feet wide—the picture is bewildering! After this we wonder at the comparative poverty of his typical mine, calculated by paltry ounces, 350 to the ton. Such giant shoots would certainly yield such ponderous masses of of gold that they would be quoted at so many hundredweights to the hundred tons of ore. We have been accustomed to hear of measurement by inches in connection with gold shoots, but we live and learn. Referring to the so-called "fissure lodes," it may be noted that these shoots invariably traverse the reef diagonally, accompanied by parallels, and they owe their origin to replacement and not fissure. No doubt there are found occasionally fissure veins in which gold occurs in bunches, but these have no regularity in this direction, and are simply the result of packing against some opposite medium. Although extremely profitable when found, this formation is not of a very permanent nature, and will "cut out" when least expected; whereas the more reliable shoot or string gold, when it does "cut out" at one spot, probably will "cut in" at another. Up to this point "Australia" has taught us nothing; nay, he has—no doubt unconsciously—sought to mislead us.

We next arrive at what the writer is chiefly driving at, namely, that the Stock Exchange should appoint "one or two disinterested and thoroughly reliable and practical men to vouch for the reports made on the different mines on the field; examine the property as compared with the reports, and either modify or attest the truth of the same." Now "Australia's" suggestion would have been more practical if he had given us the names of one or two such prodigies of integrity as he describes. Possibly he would undertake the job himself. It would have kept him busy of late rushing from Coolgardie to Murchison and thence on to Pilbarra; but would it, as he asserts, "save endless misery and losses to the investing public ?"

Another correspondent of the *Pall Mall Gazette*, who signs his own name, and has pitched his tent in Old Broad Street, joins issue with "Australia" for imputing a lack of intelligence to the investing public. Mr. Arthur E. Ritchie sees no necessity for tendering investors gratuitous advice, and thinks that ample guarantee is already provided by the "competent and reliable experts sent out from here on behalf of certain London firms." The worst of it is that these gentry, even supposing them to be competent and reliable, cannot be expected to be disinterested, receiving as they do payment from the London firms in question, and very frequently having a direct personal interest in the properties they report upon. We very much doubt, therefore, if, as this confident correspondent states, "the general public may rest assured that the ventures they are asked to subscribe to have *bonâ fide* prospects of success," so long as they bear the sign manual of these immaculate representatives of certain London firms.

The investing public should indeed feel grateful for this friendly counsel, diametrically opposite as it happens to be. Investors will find it hard to know which advice to take. We venture to suggest a safe alternative. Be advised by neither one nor the other, and put not your trust in *experts*.

XXIX.—DECLINED WITH THANKS.

No subject connected with the welfare of Western Australia interests us more deeply than exploration. We are so fully assured of the immense resources contained within the vast area of the Colony, that we heartily welcome any work which tends to reveal her riches to the world. We therefore confess to feeling considerable regret when we learn that the offer made by Mr. Clarence D. Brown to give his services gratuitously for the purpose of leading an exploring party through the hitherto untrodden regions of the interior of Western Australia has been refused. We do not, of course, pretend to question the wisdom of Sir John Forrest's action in the matter. On the contrary, we feel convinced that he was actuated by the highest motives; nevertheless, we are sorry that he could not see his way to recommending the House to sanction the undertaking.

There can be no doubt that the combination of a scientific Government survey, with an inspection of the natural features of the interior, is at all times desirable; and such a system could hardly fail to commend itself to so celebrated an ex-official of the Survey Department as the Premier, who, as is well-known, has gained for himself imperishable laurels in the field of exploration. Certainly some of the most successful expeditions have been led by distinguished members of the Survey Department. Our mind naturally reverts to Mr. George Evans, who, in 1813, discovered the Lachlan and Macquarie

Rivers, together with that magnificent agricultural and grazing country known as Bathurst Plains. A few years afterwards, John Oxley—the Surveyor General of New South Wales—conducted several expeditions of great importance, with conspicuous skill and success. Captain Charles Sturt, who held the same high post in the Survey Department, stands in the very front rank of Australian explorers. Sir Thomas Mitchell, also Surveyor General, was probably the most successful of all the explorers, having the good fortune to discover Australia Felix— that magnificent territory which became the rich colony of Victoria. The heroic Kennedy, whose sad fate in 1848 cast a gloom over the Colony, was a martyr to the cause of exploration ; and many other officials of the Survey Department have, in the same line, rendered inestimable service to Australia.

Mr. Brown takes rather an injured and indignant attitude in consequence of his offer being declined. It is a pity that he should do so ; for it gives one the impression that he wishes to force his services upon the country. No doubt it is a somewhat painful position to be placed in, but unfortunately anyone who tenders himself for such a position, lays himself open to refusal. He is certainly dogmatic in his utterances ; "I contend," he writes, "that an undertaking of this kind is absolutely necessary for the well-being and prosperity of the country." Sir John, on the other hand, after thanking him for his offer, says : "There does not appear to me to be any necessity for such an expedition at the present time." A pretty decided difference of opinion, one would say; and we fear there can be but one answer to the question, "Whether should Sir John, or Mr. Clarence Brown, be the more capable of judging in the matter?"

The latter gentleman seems to think that the Premier had no right to take upon himself to refuse his offer, which was made "to the people of Australia." He is aggrieved because it was not laid on the table of the House, for the consideration of the representatives. It would have been somewhat absurd, we think, for Sir John to lay a proposition before the House which he could not recommend, nor endorse, and moreover, it is just possible that Mr. Brown's feelings would have been even more severely ruffled had the Premier taken this course.

If our memory serves us right, a two years' trip into the interior is a record-breaker as to the length of time. The disastrous Burke and Wills' Expedition was provisioned for twelve months, the weight of these supplies amounting to twenty-one tons. The leader, Robert O'Hara Burke, was an enthusiastic volunteer. The subscriptions, together with a Government subsidy of £5,500, amounted to £8,500, which makes us doubt whether Mr. Brown had not under-estimated the cost of this two years' tour of investigation. We do not suppose, however, that he contemplated fifteen men and twenty-four camels.

Now that the proverbial cold water has been thrown upon the proposition by Sir John and his colleagues—for we think it highly probable that he consulted his brother Ministers—there is nothing left for Mr. Brown, but either to find a dozen men of like mind with himself ready to work for nothing and start off, or on the other hand to enlist the sympathies of those who can and will supply the sinews of war. We wish him all success. The proprietor of this journal, intends issuing a work on the Exploration of Australia, and will welcome any new facts regarding the great problems of the interior. Unfortunately, however, his book will probably be out before Mr. Brown is, and therefore his pilgrimage can scarcely be chronicled in the first edition. Seriously, we are sorry that this expedition is not to be conducted on the lines suggested. We rejoice at every new contribution to our knowledge of Western Australia, and we feel sure many interesting items of information would have been forthcoming. With the tidings of Bayley's Londonderry, and Wealth of Nations—those stars in the firmament of gold mining industry—ringing in our ears, we are more and more confirmed in our belief of Western Australia's great auriferous wealth. These properties all lie within a very small area compared with the enormous expanse of the Colony. Doubtless it is a very noble reward that has repaid the fortunate prospectors who found these great gold mines, and perhaps Sir John Forrest thinks that the probability of a good many such parcels of gold being dotted over a large portion of Western Australia will induce prospectors to gradually explore the whole territory on their own account. We are reminded of a proposition to empty a certain lake in Scotland, when a wag suggested that if a couple of barrels of whiskey were emptied into it the people would soon assemble and drink it dry!

XXX.—EX UNO : DISCE OMNES.

The immense benefit which has already resulted from the fact that Western Australia has been proved beyond cavil and question to be a gold-producing country is not to be gainsayed. No other discovery could possibly be attended with such rapid and surpassingly potent consequences to the colony. At the same time it must be admitted that a truer source of wealth lies in the cultivation of the land. This has, naturally, been recognised by the Premier of the colony, who has exhibited his foresight and sagacity by the formulation of a Land Bank scheme as an appropriate sequel to the Homesteads Act. It scarcely lies within our province to criticise colonial politics. We freely concede that such questions may more safely be confided to those residing in Western Australia, upon whom the responsibility of the government rests. We think, however, that since the Bill for a Land Bank has, apparently, so far, met with the favour of the West Australian Parliament, we may allude to it. Any scheme for judiciously making advances to farmers must receive our heartiest approval. Ever since those far off days, when the gardener, Adam, and his wife, "smiled at the claims of high descent," and founded the human race, the husbandman has been the backbone of the world.

Certainly it does seem as if there were a screw loose somewhere, when we learn that the great colony of Western Australia imports almost £600,000 worth of food stuff. This, on the face of it, is a most unsatisfactory state of affairs. Western Australia should be in a position to export produce instead of buying it from other quarters. Let us hope that the remedy may be found in Sir John Forrest's scheme. A Land Bank, however, to be successful and beneficial, should be self-supporting, and not too much under Governmental management. An over-paternal Government has too often been the ruin of seemingly hopeful measures.

Some weeks ago somebody suggested that the Colonial Government should buy a few gold mines; and by so doing abolish taxation. We ventured to point out the error of such a policy. Since then we are glad to know that several prominent government officers have become possessed of a magnificent mine with which they have every reason to be pleased. It has been aptly named by some admirer of Adam Smith, "The Wealth of Nations." These gentlemen are to be congratulated; but we can scarcely expect them to hand over their profits to the Treasury.

The eyes of the world are at the present moment turned upon Russia. Now, no two countries could be more widely divided than the country of the Czar and Western Australia. There is little in common between them: and yet it may be possible to learn a lesson from their experiment. No doubt the Western Australian Ministry are aware that Russia possesses an institution called "The Peasants' Land Bank." They are probably cognisant of the terrible struggle for existence among the tillers of the soil in that vast empire.

Where we do not seek for an example we may sometimes, with great advantage, receive a lesson. It is in vain to hope that farmers, who are subjected to vexatious and bureaucratic control, can ever become enterprising and prosperous. Let us glance for a few moments at the present position of the Land Bank of Russia, which was established about twelve years ago. The enormous size of the Muscovite Empire, and certain natural disadvantages, which she shares with Western Australia, is sufficient apology for speaking of a great country and a great colony in the same breath.

In 1885, when the Russian Bank was started—under the provisions offered—it appears that the area acquired for small farms was 750,000 acres, and an about equal amount represented the operations of 1886. But the transaction subsequently began to decline—the reason advanced being that the farmers realised grave difficulties regarding the fulfilment of the obligations into which they had entered. In ten years we learn that the entire area purchased was 4,725,000 acres; and this land was assigned to 286,500 heads of families. Unfortunately, however, £642,000 worth of plots reverted to the Land Bank, through the non-payment of the advances In fact, the condition of the smaller agricultural class became such, that the Imperial Government was last year forced into the position of passing an Act, allowing, practically, an indefinite period for the liquidation of debts. The true meaning of this measure seems to be, that debts which the farmers cannot pay, are not to be enforced. At the same time these liabilities will be kept alive in the vain hope of brighter times. A pleasant and encouraging state of affairs. Twelve millions sterling is the amount owed, and things appear to be going from bad to worse.

We take leave to throw out these few hints in the hope, and with full belief, that Western Australia will steer clear of the shoals and rocks of insolvency. Human nature is strangely alike all over the world, and the position of Western Australia a century hence may largely depend upon the wisdom of her present movements.

XXXI.—AN ADVISORY SYNDICATE.

Truly the West Australian Boom is responsible for strange developments, judging from a *private and confidential* circular which was handed to us for perusal. It is a document which should be preserved among the archives of company-promoting effrontery long after the last echoes of the "boom" have died away. The epistle in question is addressed to those fortunate "Ladies and Gentlemen" who happily possess shares in five different companies, namely :—The West Australian Gold Fields, Limited; the London and Western Australian Exploration Co., Limited; the West Australian Exploring and Finance Corporation, Limited; the West Australian Pioneer Syndicate, Limited; and the Hampton Plains Estate, Limited. These good people have apparently been thus honoured because they have been constantly besieging the offices of their respective companies with inquiries as to which new mining venture they should invest their money in. Hence the circular, which states that "of course it is quite impossible to answer every individual inquiry." So much for the recipients of this printed letter.

And now as to the writers. By a curious coincidence they happen to be Messrs. Stoneham, Thompson, Wright, Moir and Butler, which gentlemen hold respectively the positions of secretary, chairman, managing director, manager, and chairman of the above-named companies in their order of mention. There is an enclosure, too, printed in a style which would do credit to Exeter Hall, with a pretty little picture of an owl on the watch for mice by way of illustration. The idea is appropriate, especially as the bird seems ready to fly at a moment's notice. Possibly it is the crest of the associated companies. Are they on the watch for the deadly bogus? Perhaps so. Still the owl is a Bird of Prey, which gives our thoughts an unhappy turn.

To resume. The "Ladies and Gentlemen" already referred to are invited to give the enclosed tract their "very careful consideration." It is an account of an interview with Mr. C. A. Moreing, which appeared in the *Mining World and Engineering Record* of October 20th. With this individual's views it appears that this newly-constituted Advisory Syndicate "thoroughly agree." Like Pilate, they asked "What is truth?" More fortunate than Pilate, the answer came in the shape of Mr. Moreing. But why, we ask ourselves, should these disinterested mentors so thoroughly coincide in their views with Mr. Moreing? A glance at the enclosure reveal why this disinterested Mining Engineer has been stamped with the hall mark of veracity. The interviewer has asked him, "Will you tell the public how to discriminate between the good and the bad," how to separate the sheep from the goats and so forth. Whereupon the Oracle speaks. These are his words as reported:—"To discriminate between good and bad companies requires but the application of simple rules, four in number. First, avoid any company that only has vendors' reports to recommend the property to be acquired. Unless the directors of a company have been sufficiently careful to obtain an independent report, and are sufficiently honest when it has been obtained to act upon it, avoid that company as you would a plague. That is the first rule, and the second is like unto it:— Avoid companies which are floated largely on the strength of a famous mine adjoining. They are generally swindles. You will see some of these West Australian prospectuses with no allusion to the property which the company is to acquire, but every allusion to some valuable property adjoining, which belongs to somebody else. Whilst giving, in all the glories of large type and glowing language a description of these adjoining properties, they are careful to avoid saying anything about the property that is being offered. Thirdly, you must see that respectable directors and engineers are in charge, men who would not permit a company to be floated without a well-examined—independently examined property, and a sufficiency of working capital. Fourthly, ascertain that the company is brought out under respectable auspices. *There are several companies now engaged in West Australian business that have able and trustworthy representatives on all the various gold fields. The public may be sure that anything bearing their stamp is genuine. The chief of these are the West Australian Gold Fields, Limited; the London and Western Australian Exploration Co., the West Australian Exploring and Finance Corporation, the West Australian Pioneer Syndicate, and the Hampton Plains Estate."* The italics are ours. We cease to wonder why the quintette who sign the circular " thoroughly agree" with Mr. Moreing. He rushes from the general to the particular with a vengeance.

So glaring and transparent an attempt to humbug the "Ladies and Gentlemen" would be intensely amusing, if it were not extremely dangerous. The circular is admittedly *private and confidential*, italicised by the advisers. It is fervently to be hoped that most of the recipients took fright at the emblem of the "Owl," and, recognising its significance, consigned the precious document to the privacy of the waste paper basket. The unblushing impudence of the conception takes one's breath away. Surely there may be a stray mine, worth investing in, which is not engineered by the people referred to.

XXXII.—THE COMMAND OF THE SEA.

"Let me make the ballads, let who will make the laws," was a remark chronicled by Fletcher, of Saltoun. Jokes can scarcely aspire in the present day to the position held by popular poetry in the Middle Ages; still they have their place, and the New Humour, has, undoubtedly, a powerful hold on the multitude. *Like Joko*—a distinguished contemporary, lately launched on the wreck-producing sea of periodical literature—has an Australian item in his second number. We are told that since the colonials first imported camels, the animal has so much improved that the Australian quadruped is now nearly double the size of the Arabian. This is certainly very cheering, if true; but, alas, we fear that our witty friend merely makes the statement in order to make his joke. He thinks that this extraordinary development in size, owing to skilful Australian breeding, will make it awkward for camel-swallowers." We have heard of the famous camel of the German scientist, which was evolved over a study fire from the depths of the author's inner consciousness. Possibly this may be the case with the quadruped mentioned by Mr. Harry Furniss.

We are, however, grateful for the attention and compliment paid to those of our colonial brethren who have endeavoured to bring the "Ship of the Desert" up to the mark. It is a troublesome beast to rear, as we have shown more than once in these columns; moreover, it certainly would seem as though it got plenty to eat in the much talked of deserts of West Australia, so as to double its weight. Western Australia is pre-eminently a camel-country; and, doubtless, before her great area is traversed by railways, she will find abundant use for these beasts of burden.

Passing by an easy gradation of thought from ships of the desert to ships of the sea,—we are glad to observe that matters are to be so adjusted that the metropolis of Western Australia is no longer to remain in the background so far as shipping is concerned. It certainly has always appeared to us an anomaly of the first water to realise that the Western coast of the Island Continent, which, by its comparative accessibility, was first visited by vessels from the civilised world, should have fallen into obscurity for so many years after Captain Cook surveyed the Eastern shores. It is several centuries since the Western coast was chartered, and little more than a hundred years have passed since our maps contained the tracing of the other margin of Australia.

Whether the position of Perth was well selected as the capital it is too late now to enquire. One thing is certain that thousands of men have visited Albany, to whom Freemantle and Perth are merely geographical names. It is, indeed, an unfortunate state of affairs, when the seat of Government of either country or colony is in an out-of-the-way situation. Sometimes a location is incapable of remedy. Liverpool is said to have been built on the wrong side of the Mersey; still, there she is, and she has got to make the best of it. Washington is admittedly the wrong place for the seat of supreme Government in the United States; and change of locality is often discussed. The writer has frequently heard it stated that some more central point, such as Kansas City, would yet have to be selected, The Command of the Sea is a cry we often hear at the present moment. There are two distinct commands, however: those which concern War and those which concern Peace — each closely connected. The latter alone applies to Western Australia, nor is she likely to rule the waves until, perhaps, that far off future day when Lord Macaulay's New Zealander sits on London Bridge surveying the ruins of London!

Probably no item in the Loan Bill, at present passing through the Legislative Assembly of Western Australia, will commend itself more strongly to the sympathies of thinking men in either hemisphere than that £200,000 for the Freemantle Harbour Works. Although the subject has been discussed for many years, it is only within the last two years that the colony has been definitely and finally committed to the scheme. A safe and commodious harbour at Freemantle, will, undoubtedly, not only facilitate local trade, but if an anchorage is afforded where the largest ocean-going steamers can approach and enter in safety during all weathers, one more important foundation stone will have been laid upon which may be reared a great edifice of commercial and national prosperity,

Unfortunately there is a parsimonious tendency in

the Opposition, whether from honest conviction or for purposes of obstruction, we will not attempt to determine. One thing is certain—that unless the Harbour Works in every way fulfil the requirements of the case, the great steamship lines which trade to Australia will give the place a wide berth, and Perth will just be where she was so far as English and foreign commerce is concerned. Into details of the scheme it is not our province to go. It is being discussed with a certain acrimony, which would be amusing if such important interests were not involved. Some of the repartee indulged in cannot pre vail. One gentleman, however, strikes a true note when he states that the Harbour Works will be the biggest asset of the colony, and it joins the federation of Australia, inasmuch as Perth will become the Western *entrepot* of Australia.

We need scarcely say that we have every confidence that, in spite of surface difference of opinion, the weight of common sense, added to professional skill, will turn the balance in the right direction. Western Australia is in the position of commanding the very highest technical skill regarding the construction of her Harbour Works. Need we reiterate the time-worn truth that all amateur advice is fraught with danger. The Colony has leapt within a very short space of time from darkness and obscurity into the light of popularity and notoriety. She may within a few years become a very great English Colony. The extraordinary revelations of her hidden wealth bring her into fierce competition with the other great gold-producing Colony. We mean South Africa, and what detractors are pleased to term the "Western Australian Boom," naturally lays her open to jealousy, sneers, and misrepresentation. But knowing, as her legislators well know, their immense responsibilities, her vast possibilities, her indubitable wealth; and recognising the patent fact that she is destined to become the home of millions of British subjects, we feel sure that party animosity will be sunk in a desire for the general good.

With the grandeur of her prospects and the magnificence of her territory, England will look to her to help abolish the lower and too often criminal order of her crowded cities in the only way possible, namely by giving them ample opportunity of making a home beyond the seas, where they can live in comfort and cleanliness, and thus solve a problem which has for centuries disturbed the world.

XXXIII.
"BETTER TO BEAR THE ILLS WE HAVE THAN FLY TO OTHERS THAT WE KNOW NOT OF."—*Shakespeare.*

An interesting correspondence, to which we shall presently refer, recalls to mind the words of one of the giants in literature of the present century—Victor Hugo. He writes as follows :—"One day, and one not far distant, the seven nations which compose all humanity shall mix and mingle like the seven prismatic colours in one radiant bow in the heavens. And the prodigy of Peace will appear visible and eternal, high above civilisation. And the astonished and dazzled world will contemplate the gigantic rainbow of the United Peoples of Europe." So much for the text, and now for its application.

On several occasions in these columns we have stated our opinion that the co-operation of Western Australia with the other Colonies, in a scheme of Federation, was a question for future consideration. What were the actual views of her Ministry on this subject at the time we wrote ? We had no means of knowing, for certain ; but we strongly suspected that they were by no means ready to enter upon the matter just at present.

About six months ago, in our issue of May 17th, we commented upon a speech made by Sir Henry Parker, in the Town Hall, Perth, Western Australia. He was very strong on the subject of Federation; and, being the G.O.M. of Australia, he was listened to, applauded, and, of course, liberally banqueted. But we never believed that he carried conviction to the Westralian heart. He promised them great things, no doubt, even to the illumination of their coasts! She would need about 750 light-houses and light-ships on the Indian and Southern Ocean seaboard to do the job well. He also drew comparisons with the German Federation, with the United States of America, and with the Dominion of Canada. We took the liberty of pointing out that these comparisons were fallacious, and we plainly said that we thought Western Australia would be much better and safer to "paddle her own canoe" for some little time to come.

She was left severely alone so long as she was a poor, struggling, neglected territory; and in all human probability the other Colonies would have troubled themselves but little about her at all, had she not revealed her great golden dowry. Sir Henry acted his part of Agent-in-Advance to the "Federation Combination" with undoubted skill. He ventilated, advertised, and may be said to have placarded the Colony in readiness for the appearance on the boards of Mr. G. H. Reid, Premier of New South Wales.

This gentleman, in his letter to Sir John Forrest, evidently anticipates the reply which he received, and like an astute statesman he endeavours to refute in advance the main objections to Western Australia's immediate co-operation. "Urgent local questions," he writes, "have endangered the continuity of the movement." "Urgent reforms pressing for settlement, &c." And then he goes on to say that he and his colleagues believe that "Federal Union can be adopted without prejudice to the performance of these pressing obligations." In short, his letter to the West Australian Premier is a conspicuously *pressing* one.

Sir John and his colleagues saw matters from a totally different point of view. Hence, Mr. Reid gets a reply to the effect that the Western Australian Parliament is so engrossed with many pressing local concerns, *chiefly caused by the immense development of her goldfields*, that it is not possible to deal with the question.

We have, therefore, *pressing* matters in both Colonies : those of New South Wales can be set aside in favour of Federation, but those of Western Australia are paramount, and Federation must be shelved indefinitely until they are disposed of. We fully coincide with Sir John Forrest's action in the matter, and it is with some gratification that we turn over the back numbers of the *West Australian Review*, and find that six months ago we prophesied his action.

It may be instructive, in this connection, to glance back three years and four months into the pages of a very great and influential London periodical, viz., *The Nineteenth Century*. In July, 1891, Mr. G. H. Reid, M.P., held rather different (at least, much modified) opinions on the question of Federation. Very different indeed from those expressed in the letter to which we have referred, which is dated 22nd August, 1894. Here are his words in the latter document :—" Indeed, it appears to us, even from the most strictly provincial points of view, that the establishment of a Federal compact is of commanding interest to every Australian State ; for it is clearly impossible that any one of them can have full scope for the development of its resources until the whole Continent is freed from provincial trade restrictions, &c., &c." So much for his opinion about two months ago. What do we find him writing to the *Nineteenth Century?* We quote from his article on "The Commonwealth of Australia." "The vast progress of these Colonies will not be seriously retarded by the failure for a time of the Federal movement. The emulations and rivalries of the individual Colonies have led to some evils, but, animating each, they have vastly stimulated the progress of all. Far removed from serious danger without, and safe from anarchy within, they are not called on, happily, to legislate in a panic. Extensive vistas of pioneer work still meet the eye on every side. There is ample virtue still in the movement which decentralised government in Australia. These Colonies can exist separately with less inconvenience than any other group of communities. Each has a seaboard hundreds of miles long, and, excepting Victoria, the smallest is larger than England and France combined. There is not a single land boundary to defend against a foreign neighbour, and their chief ports, far from the central region of hostile demonstrations, can easily be made impregnable." That there may come a time when it will be to the advantage of Western Australia to join in a Federation Union with the other Colonies, there cannot be a shadow of doubt. But her present position has been achieved under separate government. Moreover, she has only had four years' experience of her New Constitution. Her wealth of gold is only in the early dawn of its development. She has long independently conducted her affairs with wisdom and success. Her credit has been sound. Her banks have steered clear of the shoals of insolvency. Well, then, may she decide to bide her time before entering into the Commonwealth of Australia!

XXXIV.—A PRODUCT OF JOINT STOCK ENTERPRIZE: THE PROMOTER.

Our humorous American contemporary, *Puck*, defines a Promoter as "a man who sells something he hasn't got to people who don't want it." This may be true in certain cases, and especially so under the Stars and Stripes. But just as there are "new laid eggs" and "shop eggs," so there are promoters and promoters. Some of these gentry are undoubtedly very bad eggs; and strange to say that these eggs are hatchers instead of *hatchees*, inasmuch as their business is the hatching of public companies; and in truth these are a motly brood.

It often happens that there is an individual known as the Exploiter or Vendor. He has a property of some sort to dispose of—it may be a mine, or it may be some scheme, imaginary or real; or, indeed, anything under the sun. Occasionally he approaches the investing public himself, but more frequently he applies to a promoter who conducts the delicate negotiations which arise, before the purse strings are loosened and the mare made to go.

The Promoter was called into existence by the State recognition of limited liability some thirty years ago, and his really busy time comes on when, after a lull, the public are seized with a sort of mania for rushing into speculations of all kinds—good, bad and indifferent. Generally the two latter adjectives are applicable. Some will remember a very big concern called the Credit

Foncier; and many of our subscribers will recollect the enormous sums squandered upon the Imperial Land Company of Marseilles, by this wealthy institution. Then what happened? Before eighteen months had expired the Credit Foncier went into liquidation, while the unhappy shareholders were poorer by two millions sterling.

The investing public did not seem to profit by the lesson. There came a boom in American gold and silver mines, and a severe lesson was taught by the celebrated Emma Mine. Then came an Indian mining mania, and afterwards the diamond and gold mines of South Africa.

It is said with truth that the manipulation of prospectuses is not such a flourishing industry as was the case twenty years ago; nevertheless, last year, no fewer than 2,617 new Companies, with a nominal capital of 112 millions (31 millions being actually subscribed) were formed.

It rarely happens that the Promoter of a Company has actually inspected the property offered to investors; and this more especially in connection with Western Australia. The reason is obvious when we consider that it is the most remote English Colony, and moreover, the gold mines are situated at great distances from the various ports of call. He gets into indirect communication with the vendor or vendors, and then proceeds to concoct a prospectus, and hunt up directors. We do not for a moment deny that, to be properly equipped for his profession, the Promoter needs to be endowed with a very level head, combined with knowledge of character;

he requires great industry, patience, and an excellent memory; for he must bear in mind the details of any scheme which he undertakes to float, be it railways, mine, manufacture, or patent.

Of course it is the gambling spirit of the public upon which he chiefly thrives, and this spirit is responsible for the more glaring abuses in the flotation of public companies. These often come to grief through going to allotment upon insufficient subscribed capital. Some are designed to take over bankrupt concerns, and are risky to a degree.

That there are genuine and honest promoters we do not for a moment deny, and our sympathies are with such as are occasionally visited with the censure of the public for sending forth highly spiced and exaggerated statements; when the real blame is attributable to the grasping Vendor, whose only motive in selling his property is to swindle the public. These cases are rare, however, and the Promoter should make sure of his facts before issuing his prospectus.

We shall welcome any legislation which will clip the wings of the fraudulent Promoter. Our interest lies with "Western Australia and its Welfare," and we have oftentimes declared in these columns, and in the writings of our proprietor and editor, that nothing would tend more to obstruct the progress of this great golden Colony, than bogus concerns forced upon the English money market.

We can only hope that our continued efforts will be more or less successful. We should be sorry indeed to see such a state of affairs in Western Australia, as is distressing her colonial sisters. We note that two of the re-constructed banks are preparing to apply to the depositors for a modification of the conditions. These two banks have engaged to pay $4\frac{1}{2}$ per cent., and are unable to do so.

But Western Australia has fortunately held aloof from the other Colonies, and has invariably conducted herself with wisdom, modesty and prudence. Thus it is that she is able to reap her golden harvest with full satisfaction, standing before the world with credit unimpaired.

XXXV.—" SUN "-LIGHT ON WEST AUSTRALIA.

"WEST AUSTRALIAN GOLD MINES.—J. T. JONES.—We quite agree. The water question is a far more serious one than has yet been admitted. The difficulties are probably not insurmountable; but they are there, and it will cost money to overcome them."

The above is among the answers to correspondents in the columns of our worthy contemporary, *The Sun.* Such answers have long been our delight. Their charming vagueness appeals to the imagination, and sets us a-wondering what the question was, and who asked it. In years gone by, we used to marvel how the giant mind of the Editor could adapt itself, either to denouncing policies, or to giving parental, legal, medical, indeed universal advice upon any subject under the sun. After hurling Olympian thunderbolts at the heads of foreign governments in one part of the paper, we have observed with amazement that "Hopeless' was advised to take a tea-spoonful of tincture of capsicums, when the craving comes on; or perhaps "Freckles" was recommended to apply a little vaseline to the part affected at bed time. Wills and testaments, pimples, canaries, dogs, love-sick damsels or home-sick school-boys—nothing seemed to come amiss to the Editor. His intellect was only comparable to an elephant's trunk, which is said to be capable either of picking up a needle or uprooting a tree. Moreover, from the tone of his answers, and his sagacious and often almost affectionate advice, we used to picture the writer of " Answers to Correspondents " as the wisest, kindliest and most benevolent of mortals. We know better now.

Of course *The Sun* knows all about Western Australia, and its answer to Mr. J. T. Jones is both interesting and instructive. Evidently J. T. has given that excellent newspaper a little bit of his mind, otherwise why those confidential and reassuring words, " we quite agree ? " We are not usually inquisitive, but we should like very much to know upon what point or points, Jones and *The Sun* agree. We may well be excused for our curiosity, for presumably he was dilating on the West Australian Water Question—that " far more serious matter than has yet been admitted." We have hitherto been labouring under the impression that it had been admitted to be a matter of surpassing seriousness and importance. *The West Australian Review* has not only admitted it, but has devoted dozens of columns to reiterating, emphasizing and insisting upon the claims of Water Supply to the most earnest attention and liberal expenditure. The West Australian press likewise have not hesitated to print the most harrowing narratives of distress and inconvenience through lack of water, and the Colonial Government have apportioned a large sum of money in order to obviate this by far the most formidable obstacle on some of the magnificent goldfields which have revealed to the world the enormous wealth of Western

Australia. We really wish that Mr. Jones could suggest something better than those devices which at present are being discussed by the Parliament at Perth.

Our concordance to Shakespeare is at the binder's, or else we should certainly look up an appropriate quotation from the "Swan of Avon" concerning this debate, for one party wishes to tap the River Swan, and another to pump water from the River Avon. Then there are those who, looking upon these methods as too costly, roundly abuse the present boring apparatus at present being used, and who declare that nothing but a diamond drill will penetrate the earth's crust deep enough to reach the subterranean waters. "Percussion drills," says these experts, "are all very well for cutting through the tertiary and mesozoic or secondary rocks: but where the older rocks, and igneous or plutonic dykes are encountered, they are utterly useless." They go on to tell us that the archœan crystalline or azoic rocks defy the very finest of steel tools, and that endless time is lost in drawing and replacing the rods, sharpening the drills and so forth. Nothing short of the diamond drill will do the work according to their opinion. It has accomplished its object at Queensland, where an abundance of water has been obtained at a depth of between 1,200 to 2,000 feet; why not at Coolgardie? Why not, indeed?

But again we are met with the flat and disheartening assertion that there is no water there at all, so what is the use of spending money on boring? The geological conditions of Central Australia—the great artesian water area—are quite different, it appears. That territory was at one time a huge inland sea, and to this fact is ascribed its abundance of underground water. There is, of course, a vast difference between this huge inland sea, filled up by gradual silting, and the impervious and ancient rock systems which distinguish Western Australia. We become confused. Why did Jones or *The Sun* not speak more fully ?

"That is all very well in theory," says another authority, but when in Champion Bay district I saw in one of the copper mines a vein of water running parallel by the side of a lode of ore without any inconvenience to the works until it opened, when it became impossible to stop the overpowering rush of water, which ran off in the form of a small river, and this was only eighty feet from the surface. Then, again, our most recent despatches contain the welcome tidings that a bore of 111 feet in depth, at the base of the Darling range, yields a supply of 8,900 gallons a day, and it is stated that, if carried deeper, a larger volume of water would be tapped.

Well, at all events, it is cheering to find that, according to our contemporary, "the difficulties are probably not insurmountable." And finally we learn that "it will cost money to overcome them." This we suspected ourselves; but it is pleasant to be corroborated by so high an authority. Full well we know that the cackle of oof-bird must be heard in the land before anything of consequence is done in Western Australia or elsewhere.

One thing is certain, that whether from the Swan or the Avon, whether from the diamond drill or the percussion drill, well, tank or catch-dam—water *must* be obtained for the goldfields of Western Australia, and the sooner the authorities agree upon some scheme the better. Coolgardie having been so far proved to be the richest field, and also the district most destitute of water, naturally demands the first attention. Some of the fields, which will ere long be opened up, present no water difficulty. To call Western Australia, as a whole, a waterless country, is a libel. Long before gold was known to be in any part of the continent, when the Western Colony was yet young—so far back as 1837, Lieutenant (now Sir George) Grey conducted an expedition through the country, about Hanover Bay, and discovered among other things the Glenelg River. He had found some difficulty in procuring water for his schooner the *Lynher*, and in his journal (vol. i., page 107), on the 21st of December, 1837, he wrote these words: " This difficulty of watering only arose from the lowness of the tides, and our ignorance of the country. Subsequently we found no difficulty in procuring it. Indeed, no country in the world is better watered than this part of Australia."

As we go to press we learn through Reuter's agency that Parliament was prolonged by Sir W. F. C. Robinson, the Governor, on the 5th instant, and that all the bills submitted by the Government have been passed. What most concerns us, however, in connection with the foregoing remarks, is the statement that a sum of £70,000 was voted for the development of the goldfields, and that Parliament subsequently authorized the expenditure of a further similar amount. We do not for a moment suppose that any river-tapping operations are contemplated in this vote. Either one or other would of course require a separate loan, unless some scheme could be devised which would enable private enterprise to undertake the work. Nevertheless £14,000, wisely spent, will do much towards the development of the goldfields; and if the sum should be inadequate to the full accomplishment of its object, such splendid results will have been shown as will simplify and facilitate raising of all further necessary capital.

XXXVI.—AUDI ALTERAM PARTEM.

In our issue of November the 29th we printed an extract from *Truth*, entitled "A West Australian Scandal." It had reference to a dispute between the Government of Western Australia and the Great Southern Railway Company of that Colony. The *casus belli* was certain land to be granted to the Company in lieu of subsidy. The Colonial Judge non-suited the Company—who, it is stated, appealed to the Privy Council—the result of such appeal being judgment on all points for the Railway Company. "Will it be believed," asks *Truth*, "that the Prime Minister of Western Australia now refuses to bow to the decision of the Privy Council?" So far as we are concerned, our plain answer is "No; it will not be believed."

On a certain Friday, in the spring of *Anno Domini* 33, Pontius Pilate asked the question, "What is Truth?" It was a standing conundrum among the ancients. Plato said we could know Truth if we could sublimate our minds to their original purity. Arcesilaos said that man's understanding is not capable of knowing what Truth is; Gorgias the Sophist said, "What is right, but we prove to be right. What is Truth, but what we believe to be Truth." Now we in these latter days have the advantage of Pontius Pilate and Company. We knew, for example, that *Truth* is sixpence, and we likewise have heard that it is stranger than fiction.

Now it would be really funnier than the funniest fairy tale if it were really the case that Sir John Forrest, who has so recently accepted his title on the understanding that he was to be "a good and faithful knight," had suddenly taken it into his head to defy the Imperial Government. Jack, the Giant-Killer, might well hide his diminished head. It would, indeed, be a bad case of *quem deus vult perdere prius dementat.* In short, we cannot contemplate the affair at all unless from a hypothetical point of view.

We have only heard one side of the question, and, although we are assured by the representatives of the Railway Company in London, that the Premier has taken up this reckless attitude of defiance, we should be extremely sorry to give our opinion until Sir John Forrest's version of the story. His alleged action is so very unlike what the man might be expected to do, that we do not hesitate to say that there is a misunderstanding somewhere. His worst enemies will surely give him credit for rather more than the average allowance of that uncommon commodity called common sense; and it will require more than a newspaper paragraph, or even the assertion of an accredited representative of the Great Southern Railway of Western Australia, to convince us that the Premier has taken complete leave of his wits. No; we know something of Sir John, and we know nothing of the city editor of *Truth*, nor the source of his information. What the latter says may be the truth, but is it "the whole truth, and nothing but the truth?" We scarcely think so.

Truth supposes there are "means for bringing obstinate Colonial statemen to their bearings." Our contemporary is quite correct in this supposition: There are ample means, not that we anticipate for one moment that such means will have to be resorted to. Had Western Australia really meant to resist England, the Defences Vote would not have been struck out of the estimates. We do not look forward to another Saratoga yet awhile; nay, we fervently hope that we have seen the last of insurgent Colonies. Whatever the British Government commands within the lines of the constitutional relationship between England and her dependencies *must* be obeyed. We do not dare to say that our law is perfect, or that our ideas of justice are infallible: but we do most firmly believe that, until we stand before the Judgment seat of the Great Architect of the Universe, we shall never see a nearer approach to fair and equitable treatment than under the jurisdiction of Her Majesty Queen Victoria.

We throw out the foregoing suggestions in the hope that the Colonial Government will see to it that no possible grounds may exist for such rumours, whether true or false. The present is perhaps the most critical period in the history of Western Australia up till now; and she must avoid even the appearance of evil. She has independent Government, great amplitude of territory, almost inexhaustible tracts of fertile, but hitherto untouched, soil, immense beds of coal, and mighty stores of metallic wealth; these must all be judiciously and fully developed. And when we examine the character of her people, we see fearless energy, sturdy determination, combined with a splendid spirit of enterprise. Let us hope that self-aggrandisement and unworthy jealousy may never be allowed to intrude their fatal presence upon so fair and promising a prospect; and let us further hope that all the acts of the Colonial authorities may be impartial and above suspicion, so that with well doing they may put to silence the ignorance of foolish men. Men and money Western Australia needs, and these she will get if she preserves her good name untarnished, and her credit unimpaired.

XXXVII.—A VAIN REGRET.

In a recent number of *The Sun*, under the title of "A Study in Polynesia," Mr. T. P. O'Connor expresses his regret that England, and not France, should have undertaken the gigantic task of colonizing the world. He has been reviewing and contrasting three books :—" By Reef and Palm." By Louis Becke. (London : T. Fisher Unwin). "Le Marriage de Loti," by Pierre Loti. (Paris : Calmann Lévy), "Island Nights' Entertainment." By Robert Louis Stevenson. (London : Cassell and Company). In the course of his criticism he writes :—" Is there not something to make one a little ashamed in the contrast between the brutal, unrehearsed, barbarous brutality of the English scenes, and the tenderness, sobriety and poetry of the French ?" Such a coarse, brutal, drunken nation as England sets a bad example to her dependencies : and France, however wicked, being so much more refined, romantic, and picturesque in her ways, would have made a much better mother country. This may or may not be Mr. O'Connor's real reason for casting a shade of doubt on the wisdom of Almighty Providence in ordaining that England should colonize the globe. One thing is certain, that had France colonized America, Australia, and other English-speaking dependencies, the hand of His Holiness, the Pope, would have been materially strengthened.

As a matter of fact, however, it is by the merest chance that Australia fell into the hands of the British; for, as he sailed out of Botany Bay in order to plant the Union Jack on the shore of Sydney Cove, Capt. Arthur Phillip, first Governor of New South Wales, espied two French ships, *l'Astsolabe* and *la Bussole*, under the command of the unfortunate La Perouse, sailing into the Bay with the object of securing the country for the people of France.

French names abound on the Australian coasts, resulting from the voyages of De Bougainville, De St. Alouarn, Bruny, D'Entrecastean, Baudin, and others, and even so lately as 1826, General Sir Ralph Darling, Governor of New South Wales, despatched Major Lockyer with detachments of the 39th Regiment to assert (if need be) the supremacy of his Britannic Majesty in Western Australia. The site of a township was, at that time, chosen at Albany, which was held as a military station for two years, when the Colony was formally handed over to Captain James Stirling, the first Governor of Swan River Settlement.

We take leave to differ *in toto* with the author of this unpatriotic regret. The French nation were never cut out for colonists. Their country is quite large enough to hold them, and they seem to have acquired the art, science, or handicraft—we know not which—of limiting the size of their families, and so preventing an inconvenient increase of population. England knows nothing of these methods as a nation. She is small but prolific, and needs mighty areas of land across the seas upon which to plant her sturdy sons and daughters. After all, however, it does not particularly matter what any one regrets; England possesses by far the largest area of land of any nation in the world, and it looks as if she was very likely to retain her vast possessions.

www.ingramcontent.com/pod-product-compliance
Lightning Source LLC
Chambersburg PA
CBHW020301170426
43202CB00008B/459